WJEC GCSE
ENGLISH LANGUAGE

Authors
Paula **Adair**
Gavin **Browning**
Jamie **Rees**
Jane **Sheldon**

Series Editor
Gavin **Browning**

DYNAMIC LEARNING

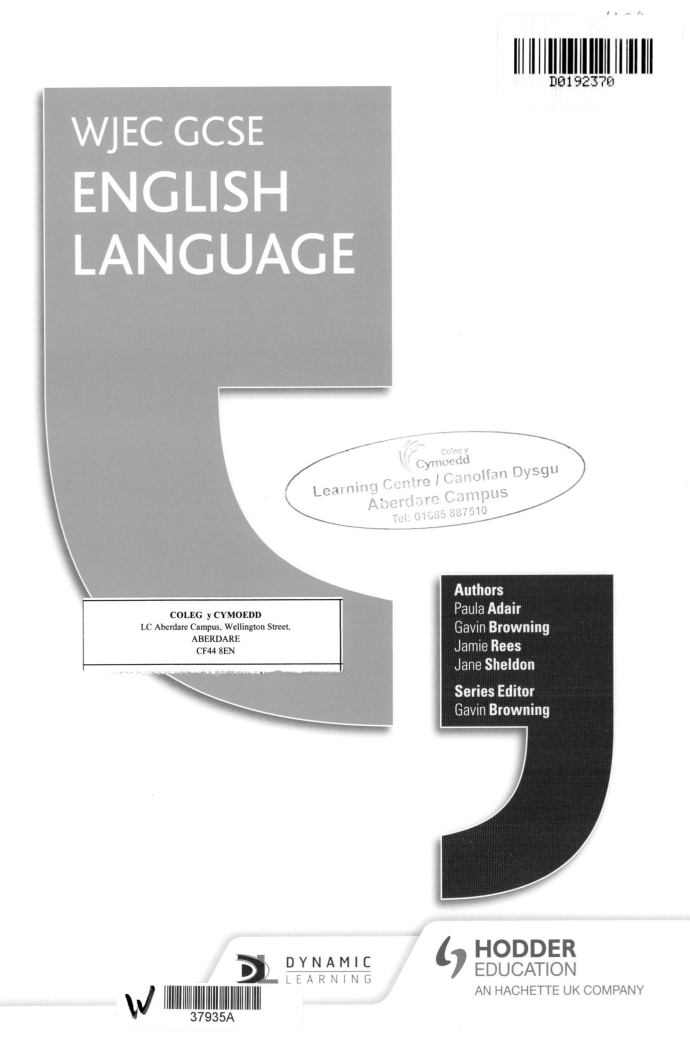

HODDER
EDUCATION
AN HACHETTE UK COMPANY

This material has been endorsed by WJEC and offers high quality support for the delivery of WJEC qualifications. While this material has been through a quality assurance process, all responsibility for the contents remains with the publisher.

Photo credits and text acknowledgements can be found on pages 180–2.

Orders: please contact Bookpoint Ltd, 130 Park Drive, Milton Park, Abingdon, Oxon OX14 4SE. Telephone: (44) 01235 827720. Fax: (44) 01235 400454. Email education@bookpoint.co.uk Lines are open from 9 a.m. to 5 p.m., Monday to Saturday, with a 24-hour message answering service. You can also order through our website: www.hoddereducation.co.uk

ISBN: 978 1 471 868351

© Gavin Browning, Paula Adair, Jamie Rees and Jane Sheldon 2016

First published in 2016 by

Hodder Education,
An Hachette UK Company
Carmelite House
50 Victoria Embankment
London EC4Y 0DZ

www.hoddereducation.co.uk

Impression number   10 9 8 7 6 5 4 3 2 1

Year   2020 2019 2018 2017 2016

Cover photo © K3/Ikon Images/Getty Images

Illustrations by Integra Software Services and Barking Dog

Typeset in 11/13pt DIN Light by Integra Software Services Pvt. Ltd., Pondicherry, India

Printed in Italy

A catalogue record for this title is available from the British Library.

Contents

Introduction

This student book is designed to improve your skills in the three Assessment Objectives of the new WJEC GCSE in English Language: Oracy, Reading and Writing. The book can be used throughout your course and contains guidance on how to improve your performance and become exam ready.

For the new GCSE you will take one non-exam assessment (Unit 1) and two exams (Units 2 and 3). Unit 1 will assess Oracy skills and Units 2 and 3 will assess Reading and Writing skills.

The book is structured thematically to help put the material in real-life contexts and give cohesion to the wide variety of texts and tasks you will meet during the course. The themes are:

* Wales
* Leisure
* The world of science and technology
* The world of work
* Citizenship.

These five themes are based on those covered in the Oracy assessments. Please note that these themes are not specified for Units 2 and 3.

Each sub-section includes (in this sequence):

1 **Oracy activities** that encourage the skills and contexts that will be assessed in the Individual Researched Presentation and Responding and Interacting tasks for Unit 1. These include opportunities to convey information or personal experiences, as well as verbally reason and persuade others.

2 **Reading activities** which help to develop the skills required in Units 2 **and** 3. These end with a more extended response question (*Compare, Analyse, Impressions etc.*) with guidance on how to perform on these 'higher tariff' tasks. This is supported by shorter response questions which build up the skills required for the new specification (*Sequencing, Multiple choice, Cloze exercises*). This sequencing of tasks prepares you for the structure of the new GCSE English Language examinations.

3 **Writing activities** which help to develop the skills required in Units 2 **or** 3. These will end with an exam-style question with sample responses, plans or scaffolds to help you to succeed in your GCSE. These sections also include proofreading activities, which again prepares you for the new specification. The **objectives** box at the start of each section clearly identifies which Unit of the exam the writing task links with.

There is also an additional chapter ('Busting the jargon') to guide you through some of the new terms and skills that apply to the WJEC English Language specification, with explanations of some of the technical words that may be used to refer to language.

Oracy

Learning objectives
In this unit you will be:
- interacting with others;
- drawing ideas together;
- responding to others' questions.

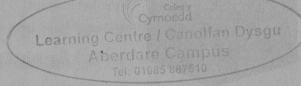

Activity 1

You have been asked to plan an itinerary for an older relative from Australia who is coming to Wales for the first time. She will only have time to see three attractions as she is here for a long weekend.

Look at the following attractions. Which three places would you choose?

Think about:
- what she wants to get out of the weekend;
- answers to any questions your cousin may have;
- distances and costs for the attractions.

Experience international rugby in Cardiff
There's little argument that rugby international weekends in Cardiff are something very special to savour, if you're going to the match, or just enjoying the atmosphere in the Welsh capital. (Cost from £45)

www.visitwales.com

Mountain Zoo
Enter the world of the Welsh Mountain Zoo and you enter a world of natural wonder. As one of North Wales' top attractions, high above Colwyn Bay with panoramic views and breathtaking scenery, its beautiful gardens are home to this caring conservation zoo. (Cost £12.10)

Crafty museums
The nimble-fingered exploits of Welsh creators is also something to savour: Newtown Textile Museum, housed in an early 19th century weaving shop, follows the process of wool to yarn and tanning to clog-making….(Cost £1.00)

Welcome to Laguna Health & Spa, Cardiff
Situated in the heart of the city centre, The Laguna Health and Spa prides itself on the array of services we offer, whether you are looking to achieve specific fitness goals in our state of the art gym, participate in one of our group exercise classes, relax in our stainless steel ozone friendly pool and spa area or pamper yourself in our Elemis and Dermologica Premier Spa. (Cost for spa day £65)

www.lagunahealthandspa.com

An adventure in space and time...

Climb aboard the TARDIS - the real TARDIS - as used by Doctors Matt Smith, David Tennant, John Hurt and now Peter Capaldi! (Cost £14.00)

www.doctorwho.tv

Conwy Castle, North Wales

Perched on a rock against the backdrop of Snowdonia, Conwy has an indisputably magical feel. Some consider it the finest castle Edward I built, and the mesmerising views from the battlements are particularly famed within the walled town... (Cost: £6.75)

www.visitwales.com

Activity 2

1 In **pairs** discuss your choices. Can you come to some agreement on the three most suitable places? Try to put your view forward by referring to the details in the texts.

2 In groups of four take on one of the following 'family' roles to ensure that your relative gets a good experience:

Your role is to:	Your role is to find out:
• set the agenda • set the timing • decide on the next steps • keep everyone focusing on the task • keep order if people disagree • handle the summary and conclusions • clarify and ask for decisions.	• What information is available? • What other information would we like to have? • What information is missing from the attraction summaries? • The pros and cons of each attraction – look at both sides.
Your role is to consider:	Your role is to put forward:
• What could be the possible problems of any of these attractions? • What aspects of the attractions might not appeal to your relative? • What things should we be cautious about – think about cost and distance?	• the benefits of each attraction • the positive feelings your relative will experience from each attraction • any savings or extra value from each event • the advantages of each attraction • how your choices can be 'sold' attractively to your relative.

Activity 3

When you have completed the discussion, present your itinerary (Friday, Saturday and Sunday) to the rest of the class. Give clear reasons for your choices.

Stretch

From the information provided prepare a spoken 'pitch' for a Tour Coach company. The pitch must try to sell the benefits of your chosen attractions. Remember to:
• use a wide range of vocabulary
• vary your tone as appropriate for a sales pitch
• avoid grammar slips, e.g. 'They **was** great'
• vary your sentences when you speak.

Reading

Activity 4

Look at the texts below. Fill in the Form, Purpose and Audience columns for these (the first one has been done for you):

Text:	Form	Purpose	Audience
Text A	Website (journey planner)	Advises and informs about world cup matches	Tourists, sports fans
Text B			
Text C			
Text D			

Text A: Welcome to the Rugby World Cup 2015 Spectator Journey Planner

Use our bespoke Journey Planner to work out your journey to any match, Fanzone or anywhere else you need to go before or after the match. You can:
- Plan trips in advance
- Get *Door to Gate* journey instructions
- Link to train, park and ride and coach booking sites directly so you can book travel in advance
- Save, print and share journey details ready for the big day

www.journeyplanner.rugbyworldcup.com

Text C: How to Surf

Part 2 of 3: Getting Started

While lying on the board, bring your hands up from paddling and place your hands below your chest, palms on the flat of the board while your fingers curl over the sides of the surfboard.

In one quick motion, push your body up with your arms and tuck your feet up and under you. Place one foot where your hands pushed up from and the other at least a shoulder's width behind.

Text B: Bring the kids along to our Soft Play Shack!

Our awe-inspiring Wavegarden lagoon isn't the only reason to come to Surf Snowdonia.

We've also given some serious thought to how we can keep our youngest visitors busy and entertained too. And we reckon toddlers and children under 12 are going to have a whale of a time in our sea-themed indoor Soft Play Shack.

www.surfsnowdonia.co.uk

Text D: What is coasteering?

Probably the best liquid refreshment in the world. Or extreme rockpooling. Or an aquatic nature-trail. In a nutshell it is an all-in-one experience that treats the foreshore as an eco-adventure playground. It's about rock-hopping, shore-scrambling, swell-riding, cave-exploring and, yes, cliff-jumping. But it's as much about discovering our wildlife and coastline at close-quarters; an intimacy that walkers never experience.

www.visitwales.com

Activity 5

1 The information in Text A refers to 'bespoke'. **Select** one definition from the list below that best defines this word:
   a Through the spoken word
   b Adapted for a specific user or purpose
   c Excellent
   d Has lots of uses.

2 Look at Text B. **Identify** two reasons why visitors should come to Wavegarden lagoon.

3 Look at Text C. **Organise** these actions into the correct sequence:
   a Place your feet under your body
   b Place your hands on the board
   c Use your arms to push your body up
   d Paddle with your hands.

4 Look at Text D. **Explain** what is meant by 'an intimacy that walkers never experience'.

Activity 6

Look at the words in **bold** from the activity above. Three of these words are asking you to **organise** or **retrieve** information. What are these three key words? Which word is asking you to do more?

Activity 7

Read Text D again. How does the writer make coasteering sound exciting?

To answer the question you should try to:
a make your point about the text
b use evidence as support
c explain how this makes it seem exciting.

Stretch

Make up two **retrieval** questions for any of the texts.

Make up one question using the word **Explain**.

Top tips

Questions beginning with:
   'How does the writer...'
   'How does the text...'
are asking you to comment on the writer's **technique**. Before answering it is very important to identify the **focus** word (in this case *'exciting'*).

Sample student responses

Which one of these sample answers follow the advice given in the Top tips?

Student A

The writer makes coasteering exciting by exaggerating the benefits of the activity: 'best liquid refreshment'. This makes it appear exciting by suggesting that it is more 'refreshing' than other activities.

Student B

The writer makes coasteering sound challenging by saying how 'extreme' it is. The adjective 'extreme' makes it sound really difficult.

Student C

The writer uses lots of exciting words to show how coasteering can be fun. You can do things like 'rockpooling' or 'cliff-jumping' and you can see lots of wildlife on the activity. The writer also says it's 'the best'.

Activity 8

Read the paragraph below and then answer the questions
that follow:

*Its striking round towers make this fortress a ....(1)....classic, and
there's every chance you'll be ....(2)..... from the moment you see the
astonishing .....(3)..... which once denied Oliver Cromwell at the
end of the Civil War. Surrounded by ....(4)....., the romantic ruins
even make space for a bowling green.*

1 Select the word which best fits the gap:

1 astounding	singular	small	run-down
2 enraptured	bored	confused	tempted
3 clouds	paintwork	gatehouse	people
4 visitors	sheep	fields	gift-shops

2 What audience is targeted at in the above text? Underline any
key words that tell you about the audience.

Top tips

Aim to use:

1 More dynamic verbs –
phrases like 'take in' and
'look out for' are not very
energetic!

2 More exciting and
informal adjectives –
for example, describing
words like 'folkloric' and
'atmospheric' can be
replaced by more energetic
words.

Activity 9

You are the editor of the Visit-Wales website and you want to attract
a younger and more energetic audience to the castles of Wales.
How would you alter the following descriptions?

Dinefwr Park and Castle

This Natural Trust-run, folkloric
12th century castle is hugely
atmospheric. Wonderful views
and guided tours take in the
nearby nature reserve, cottages,
ponds, a croquet lawn and a tea
room. Look out for the rutting
deer and cows who might join
you during a stroll around the
18th century landscape park.

Caldicot Castle

Every view from this incredible
medieval castle could be
a picture postcard, and its
history is the stuff of legend
from Norman beginnings, to
conflict in the Middle Ages, and
Victorian domesticity. Fifty-five
acres of country park await,
as well as events such as
reenactments and a tearoom
for unwinding.

Top tips

This question is asking you to find information from each text, but is not asking you to compare them. This is essentially a **synthesis** task. Here, the best approach is to tackle one bullet point at a time.

The first bullet point tells you that the focus is on '**interesting** things **to see**'. With this clear focus in mind, spot as many things as you can in **both texts** that relate to this focus. It will be easier to tackle each text separately, e.g. 'In Family Fun, you can see "Banquo the earless dog", and…'.

Once you have spotted a range of things on each text, move on to the second bullet point.

Activity 10

Now look at both texts below. What does each text tell you about what you can do there? Comment on:
- what interesting things there are to see;
- what activities you can do. [10]

Family Fun

There is plenty for children to do when you visit Cardiff Castle, from special events throughout the year and workshops to keep them busy during the holidays to trails around the grounds and through the Apartments.

Follow the Family Trail around the grounds and meet some of the characters that have made Cardiff Castle their home over the centuries. Find the answers to the questions all around the Castle with a little help from Gwen the Celtic Girl, Marcius the Roman Soldier and many more. Be sure to bring an audio guide with you or download the app to hear their stories. Once you have answered all the questions, be sure to check back here and compare your answers!

When you go inside the amazing Castle Apartments, keep an eye out for Banquo the earless dog who will start you off on the Animal Trail. Find his friends all around the house and colour in the pages of the booklet as you go.

Take a House Tour which takes you through some of the most amazingly opulent, highly decorated rooms you will ever see. Among the rooms you will visit with your expert guide are the Winter Smoking Room, The Nursery, Lord Bute's Bedroom and The Roof Top Garden. The tour runs every day on the hour and lasts approximately 50 minutes (additional charge of £3 per person)

Stretch

Evaluate the different *target audiences* of both texts.

Support your ideas by referring to the texts and using comparative words such as: *while… however… in contrast to… conversely…*

In the heart of the capital city is Cardiff Castle, a truly remarkable site with a history that spans over 2000 years. Roman soldiers slept here, noble knights held court here, and the Bute family, with extraordinary wealth and vision, transformed the Castle into a romantic Victorian fantasy. 'Eccentric genius' architect William Burges was given free rein to create the amazingly lavish and opulent interiors; each breathtaking room rich with murals, stained glass, gilding and superb craftsmanship. Recent developments include the opening of the Wartime Shelters, an evocative re-creation of a bygone era when the Castle's tunnels were used as a place of refuge during the Second World War air raids. For an alternative night out, book a traditional Welsh Banquet for your family, friends or office. This is a relaxed and fun evening of Welsh food, wine and music, in either the 15th century Undercroft or the Interpretation Centre.

A family friendly visit… Stay and play area with hands-on art and craft activities, puppet theatre and child sized costumes.

Writing

Activity 11

Look at the passage below. What is the **form**, **purpose** and **audience** of this text?

Give a reason for each of your choices.

> *Dear Sir/Madam,*
>
> *I am writing to thank you for the excellent Coasteering experience you provided for my family at the weekend.*
>
> *The organisation of the days was superb and there was never a moment that we were bored. James, my youngest child, enjoyed looking at the sealife as he swam by the rocks and my eldest son thought the 10 foot leap into the waters was 'sick'!*
>
> *As I am now well into my 40s I appreciated the concern your team showed for health and safety. While it was important I was pushed out of my comfort zone...I never once felt that the activities were out of control or would lead to my personal danger.*
>
> *Yours faithfully,*
>
> *Mr John Edwards*

Activity 12

You have been asked to rewrite this as a lively blog for people thinking of going Coasteering for the first time (you can use some of the information in Text D on page 7). What features may be more appropriate for a lively blog?

N.B. Remember, while it may be important to follow typical layout features to suit the format of a task, there is no 'checklist' of language features or content you are expected to use.

address location	*second person*	*formal register*
paragraphs	*abbreviations*	*varied sentences*
subheadings	*text speak*	*puns*
informal language	*expert opinion*	*first person*
wide vocabulary	*statistics*	
exclamations	*exaggeration*	

Sample student responses

The two articles below are responses to the following task:

You have been asked to write a lively article about an outdoor experience or activity in Wales (such as camping, hiking or canoeing, etc.) for people who are over 40 and 'don't get out much'. [20]

Think about:
- *what the activity involves*
- *the benefits of the activity*
- *how to get started.*

Surfing Wales

Fed up of looking at the telly? Want a break from the routine? Well...why not ring the changes with Surfing Wales!

What is Surfing Wales?

Surfing Wales is an organisation aimed at people thinking of hitting the waves for the first time. With our dedicated team of staff we can talk you through some of the techniques and challenges of surfing for the first time. Whether it's showing you how to land safely or keep your balance while the waves crash around you, you will be in good hands.

Why Surfing Wales?

Taking on a new skill will give you new confidence and will help you take on challenges in your life. It's also a great way of keeping fit while having fun. Getting closer to nature is, after all, a lot more interesting than trotting on the treadmill at your local gym.

How do I start?

Our team are ready to answer any of your questions on the link or phone number below.

Mountain-biking

I think mountain-biking will give you the time of your life. There are loads of exciting tracks around the countryside in Wales and ya'll never get bored when jumping over our wild tracks and swerving to miss trees and critters as you bomb it down at 110 miles an hour.

I've done mountain biking for years and it's a great way of getting the blood pumpin and getting your abs and delts sorted out for the weekend.

There are loads of good mountain-biking tracks in your 'hood. All you gotta do is get in touch with the Mountain-biking crew and they will be able to point ya in the right direction.

Once you take up the saddle you'll never look back and you know you wanna come back for more!

Which article best addresses the task? Give three reasons for your opinion.
-
-
-

Activity 13 Put it to the proof

The following article is a 'proof' for an article for a new magazine promoting Wales as a new tourist venue. There are **ten** errors below. Before this can go 'live' on a website you need to identify these errors and correct them:

> Wales is a fantastic place to visit, weather for a weekend or an extended holiday. Many of the beaches have Blue Flag awards and you can enjoy some of the most splendid sceenery that the British Isles can offer.
>
> Destinacions like Llandudno, Porthcawl and the Gower will offer something for the whole family. You can relax in the sun or take part in a range of adventure activitys around Wales rugged coastline.
>
> The capital city, Cardiff has something for everyone. Some of the regions most exotic nightlife can be found in the streets of the capital. Youll also fall in love with the arcades and boutique shops which can be found along the side avenues of the mainstream department stores.
>
> The choices of restaurants is immense. You're friends and family will love the range of cuisines to be tasted.

What sort of errors did you spot? Identify these as Spelling, Punctuation or Grammar errors below.

Stretch

Work out the rules for one of the punctuation errors. Can you explain why this is incorrect and what to do in order to avoid repeating the mistake?

Spelling	Punctuation	Grammar
e.g.rollacowster	e.g. no full stops	e.g. expression errors

Top tips

A **topic sentence starter** is usually a general, brief statement to introduce the subject matter or focus of the rest of the paragraph, e.g.

Surfing is a worthwhile challenge. *Trying to keep your balance on the water is…*

It is important to develop this statement fully. This can be done by giving real-life examples, facts, quotations or further detail.

Stretch

Look at your opening two paragraphs – how would you change the language if you were aiming your article at an older middle-aged audience?

Test yourself

Read the following exam-style question carefully:

A new tourist website 'See Wales' has asked for an article highlighting an interesting activity or place that teenagers can take part in when they visit Wales.

Write an article about an activity or attraction that you think would encourage other teenagers to go to Wales. [20]

Planning your answer

Before starting any extended writing task it is important to PLAN your response. In the exams you will be given 10 minutes of planning time and this will help you to write a more sustained and organised response. Think of four or five areas that you want to cover. Each 'area' can be turned into a **heading** or **topic sentence starter**. For example:

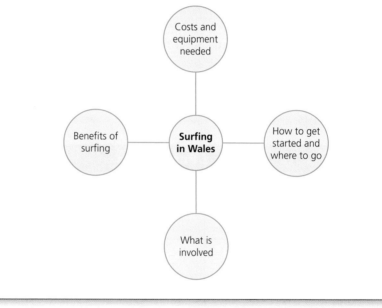

1b   In the eye of the media

Oracy

Learning objectives

In this unit you will be:
- interacting with others and drawing ideas together;
- presenting information clearly;
- improving your spoken accuracy.

Activity 1

A new Welsh TV channel (Wales View) is due to be launched next year. However, the channel executives have yet to decide which programme is going to be their 'flagship' project. This needs to be decided on by the end of the day as this programme will feature on all the new billboards and TV commercials. The creative department have highlighted some ideas for new programmes.

Which three programmes are most likely to be a success for the new channel? **Think about**:
- which show would have highest viewing figures;
- how you want to 'brand' the new channel;
- the cost and running time of the programmes.

Stretch

Using your partner as a 'listener', prepare a one-minute pitch for one of the shows. Your partner has to listen out for:
- hesitations (including 'ums' and 'OK')
- repetitions
- grammatical errors.

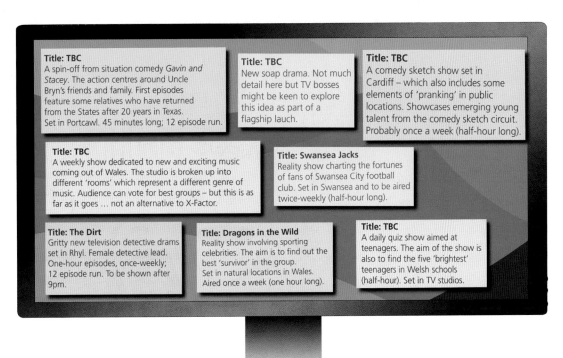

Title: TBC
A spin-off from situation comedy *Gavin and Stacey*. The action centres around Uncle Bryn's friends and family. First episodes feature some relatives who have returned from the States after 20 years in Texas. Set in Portcawl. 45 minutes long; 12 episode run.

Title: TBC
New soap drama. Not much detail here but TV bosses might be keen to explore this idea as part of a flagship lauch.

Title: TBC
A comedy sketch show set in Cardiff – which also includes some elements of 'pranking' in public locations. Showcases emerging young talent from the comedy sketch circuit. Probably once a week (half-hour long).

Title: TBC
A weekly show dedicated to new and exciting music coming out of Wales. The studio is broken up into different 'rooms' which represent a different genre of music. Audience can vote for best groups – but this is as far as it goes ... not an alternative to X-Factor.

Title: Swansea Jacks
Reality show charting the fortunes of fans of Swansea City football club. Set in Swansea and to be aired twice-weekly (half-hour long).

Title: The Dirt
Gritty new television detective drams set in Rhyl. Female detective lead. One-hour episodes, once-weekly; 12 episode run. To be shown after 9pm.

Title: Dragons in the Wild
Reality show involving sporting celebrities. The aim is to find out the best 'survivor' in the group. Set in natural locations in Wales. Aired once a week (one hour long).

Title: TBC
A daily quiz show aimed at teenagers. The aim of the show is also to find the five 'brightest' teenagers in Welsh schools (half-hour). Set in TV studios.

Activity 2

For Unit 1 you will be marked for the grammatical accuracy of your talk. Therefore it is important to avoid slips in your grammar when you are assessed for your speech.

Here are some common errors that can be made with spoken English.

Can you spot the error and correct?

- I done lots of research on this topic and I think the show would work great.
- The celebrity which does the best wins the contest.
- The local people in the first episode makes it feel real.
- I like very much the idea of an interactive quiz show.
- I been watching these shows since three years and they're great.
- She speaks really good.
- The actors didn't let down nobody on the last series.
- It's all what people like!
- Filming in summer is better as it's more hot then.

Activity 3

The Media Pitch. As Wales View's Head of New Shows you have been asked to 'pitch' a new show for the new channel.

In your presentation you need to:

- introduce the topic and purpose of your talk;
- establish eye contact with the audience throughout;
- prepare your ideas for the new show THOROUGHLY – you will need to prepare for questions about costs, actors, settings, future plots – this will be the main part of your pitch;
- explain why you think it will be a success;
- say how you would advertise the show to the viewing public;
- explain how the show might be developed in the future;
- ask for any questions.

Reading

Activity 4

Which of the following statements can be supported by the text?
- Fans are welcoming the new show *Stella*;
- The local people dislike *Stella* being filmed in their neighbourhood;
- The makers of the show do not care about local residents;
- The show has been filmed at Elm Street for at least two years.

Stella fans may be welcoming the news that the comedy drama is returning for a fourth series – but one family who live where it's filmed say 'enough is enough'.

The Sky1 programme is largely filmed in Ferndale, Rhondda, where Elm Street doubles up as the road where Stella lives.

Disgruntled dad-of-two Jeremy Hart, who lives on nearby Pine Street, says he and his neighbours are fed up with the 'major inconvenience'.

'I just feel like enough is enough. No thought whatsoever is given to other residents like myself whose lives have been made a misery over the last three years with the constant disruptions.'

(www.walesonline.co.uk)

Activity 5

Identify two facts from the text.

Activity 6

Sort these into two columns: **Facts** and **opinions**.
- The tickets for the show cost £49.00.
- The money spent at the cinema was well spent.
- The final scene was the best one in the whole movie.
- There was cheering from the audience.
- Colwyn Bay has the best scenery.
- The venue at Aberystwyth is really scary when you first go on.
- Some of the actors only eat vegetarian food.
- The show was lots of fun last night.

Stretch

Make a note of all the **evaluative adjectives** in the statements above. Replace with factual adjectives (e.g. green, round) in a way which still makes sense.

Top tips

Sometimes sorting facts and opinions can be confusing. Sometimes statements can **appear** like facts and these often use simple 'to be' verbs, e.g. 'The parrot **is** the cleverest bird in the world'. Here the **evaluative adjective** 'cleverest' is a clue that this statement is actually an opinion.

By the same token, statements that sound unsure may still be a fact, e.g. 'Cats are sometimes able to jump up to 5ft in the air.' Here the **qualifier** "sometimes" doesn't make this any less of a fact.

Activity 7

The case study below is from a report on the 'Economic Impact of S4C':

Case Study: Leverage Effect

Dream Team TV started around 15 years ago, focusing on sporting coverage for S4C. Over the years, Dream Team have employed numerous independent Welsh cameramen, utilised Welsh production facilities and raised the profile of a number of Welsh sporting events, such as the Cardiff Half Marathon which have all contributed to the economy.

Over the years Dream Team TV has expanded and now has two offices, one in Gwynedd and the other in Cirencester. Dream Team TV generates income from a number of broadcasters, and S4C's proportion of total revenue has diminished as the company has expanded into new markets. That said, Dream Team is clear that S4C's initial commissions and support (including training) were critical to the success of the company.

This provides a clear example of how S4C's initial support has enabled a Welsh firm to develop and expand, drawing in additional income from new markets.

WELSH-LANGUAGE broadcaster S4C is a 'bloated bureaucracy' that should be shut down, according to a former Conservative minister.

Rod Richards, below, who was a minister in the Welsh Office in John Major's Government from 1994 until 1996, said millions of pounds could be saved by closing the channel and transferring Welsh language programming back to BBC Wales.

He said: 'The BBC makes many of the programmes anyway. S4C makes no programmes of its own, commissioning its output entirely from others, and is a house full of administrators. The viewing figures of S4C do not justify its continued existence.'

In 2008, S4C's viewing share was 2.7% of the TV programmes watched in Wales.

Look at the statements below:
- Dream Team are an inspiration to other media companies in Wales.
- Media companies can be disloyal to S4C.
- S4C can support and encourage media companies to succeed.
- S4C loses money when companies become successful and leave Welsh broadcasting.

Try to rank order the statements in order of **how accurately they sum up** the purpose of the case study. While all the above statements may have an element of truth, this task is asking you to **evaluate** the purpose of this text.

Activity 8

Read this extract from a news article and answer the questions that follow:

1 Identify five reasons why the Conservative minister thinks that S4C should be shut down?

2 How does he try to persuade the reader it should be shut down? How are facts and opinions used?

Activity 9

You are going to read an interview with the producer of *Hinterland*, a ground-breaking detective series filmed in Welsh. Answer the following exam-style question:

*What **impressions** do we get of the TV programme? How does the interview create these impressions?* [10]

Copy and complete the table below to help you organise your ideas.

What impressions do we get of *Hinterland*?	How does the article create these impressions?
successful	*'lots of critical acclaim'* – the interviewer emphasises the success of the programme
authentic/real	

Interview: Ed Thomas, Hinterland/Y Gwyll

Hinterland/Y Gwyll is one of the UK's very best crime dramas, so the fact that it's now in full swing again (on S4C; it'll be on BBC4 later in the year) is very good news. I managed to catch up with showrunner Ed Thomas to talk about the series, and it was a really great and fascinating chat, not least because he spoke to me about his plans for the show's future:

TKT: You must be thrilled by the response to the show... it's had lots of critical acclaim but is also seen as a really strong Welsh export.
Ed Thomas: You might know better than I do! Sometimes you get so wrapped up in the bubble of making it you forget there are all kinds of interested parties out there. People who love crime, they consume it in books, films and on television. We have to compete against *True Detective* and *Fargo* and all the other great American detective shows.

TKT: You mentioned all the hard work that goes into it; does it come together quite quickly?
ET: The thing is we were careful of was the design of it and making the budget work for us. Whether you consume it in Wales or the rest of the UK or in other territories, what we're getting fed back to us is that people believe in its own kind of authenticity. The stories come out of the area and people feel the stories are about family, soil, blood, belonging... all the kind of stuff that fits with what I know about Wales. So we were really clear: the only way we could do something like *Hinterland/Y Gwyll* in both languages and make it authentic for the Welsh language audience – who are very particular – was to make it be really specific. We picked Aberystwyth in Ceredigion because we believed that Welsh is spoken enough there and the landscape... it has a big, little country feel.

TKT: This is the first time I've spoken to you so I want to take it back right to the beginning. What were you aiming for when you first came up with the idea for *Y Gwyll*? What were the kind of stories you wanted to tell?
ET: We'd already worked a fair amount in Welsh and English but S4C came on board early and pledged 40 per cent of the budget, so we had to go out and raise the rest of the finance. What we knew we had to do was find a way of exporting a version of Wales that's free of stereotypes. Historically Wales hasn't been a hotbed of drama production, for various reasons. We wanted to make sure that we could be very local but with a universal appeal. We picked on the crime drama because it's the most consumed genre globally. Secondly, we're based in Wales and we know our versions of Wales and in many way the themes that we wanted to touch on were themes that were prevalent in other works we'd done. It's kind of a love letter to a disappearing Wales, and a changing, disappearing world. When you go into Ceredigion and up into the farms there are a lot of derelict places. But what we also found were people who had moved in – hippies who had made farms with no electricity. So it's an eclectic, sort of Wild West place. The Devil's Bridge story, which we started with, was a myth, a strange and spooky real myth. Then we realised and this is probably the cleverest thing we did as a production, we went up there and reccied these places before it was green-lit with the location manager. Story two was going to be a different story, but we binned it and kept staying local – that enabled us to take the whole production up there. The most cost-effective way of doing a show like this is to keep it in, say, Cardiff, where we're based, shoot the interiors in Cardiff and then go up to Ceredigion and shoot the pretties. But if we had done that I think we would have ended up with a fundamentally different show. Whatever it costs to place us and the crew up in Ceredigion, the benefits far outweighed that cost because everywhere we looked we found an interesting theme or bits of character or a situation.

Top tips

1 Underline the key word(s) in the question.
2 Underline as much relevant evidence from the text as possible.
3 Find a **range** of points and evidence from the text.
4 Better answers will tackle **how** these impressions are created.

Sample student responses: In the exam it is very important to include a RANGE of evidence

Both the students below here have started to explain their ideas well but which one has the best RANGE of appropriate evidence from the text?

Student A

The article shows the reader how successful the show is – 'critical acclaim' – this tells us that it has received a lot of praise from the media. We also find out that the show is based closely on local stories – 'stories come out of the area' – this tells us that it would appeal to local people. The article also tells us that it is strongly Welsh as they use the Welsh language in the programme. He says that the show is 'a love letter to a disappearing Wales' which tells us that it is very important for Welsh people. The show is clearly 'based in Wales' and this is a big selling point of the programme....

Student B

The introduction suggests 'Hinterland' is 'one of the UK's very best crime dramas' – this clearly tells us it is very successful. It is also a 'very strong Welsh export' which tells us that it is not just popular in this country but has international 'acclaim'. This is very impressive as they have 'to compete' against some very strong shows from America like 'True Detective'. ET suggests they have a limited budget 'making the budget work for us' but that they concentrate on the drama being 'authentic' and focused on Welsh themes, using the Welsh language. It also focuses strongly on a 'specific' sense of place in Aberystwyth....

Writing

Learning objectives

In this unit you will be:

- adapting your style to suit form and purpose – formal letter-writing;
- paragraphing and presenting work appropriately;
- developing persuasive writing.

Activity 10

Read the following article and fill in the table with persuasive features, examples or definitions.

> *The new fat free-yoghurt from Yo-Mo tastes great, tastes awesome. We believe that this new product will explode your taste buds and change your view of yoghurts. Why would you bother eating fatty ice-creams? The quickest way of getting hold of this product is through our exclusive on-line agents. 90% of people have reviewed this on-line as a 5 star product so hurry up and go to yo-mo.com today.*

Persuasive feature	Example	Definition
Repetition	'Tastes *great*, tastes *awesome*'	
	'We *believe that...*'	
Exaggeration		
		A question that does not require an answer.
Superlatives		
	'90% of people *have reviewed this... as 5 star*'	
Imperative		

Activity 11

Spot the persuasive features in the advertisement below:

Wouldn't we all want a mobile phone that responds to your voice? This latest wrist-phone gadget will totally transform your life. The latest technology has been used to bring some fantastic touch screen features with some even more fantastic free apps for your use. But the most amazing feature is the fact that you no longer need to use your hands – a simple instruction will do it for you. Recent market research has suggested that 95% people would prefer to move towards more 'hands-free' technology. The new Watz phone is what the world has been waiting for.

Activity 12

It is very important that paragraphs are used appropriately in written texts. In persuasive letters it is important that each paragraph deals with a new topic or idea. Read the following letter, which is complaining about a new programme, and identify the 'topic area' of each paragraph (these are jumbled up down the left-hand side):

112 Wandsworth St

Cwmaman

Sign off with your name

Cynon Valley

CF44 8EW

Introduce purpose of letter

CwmMedia

7 Rumpole St

Cardiff

Offer of a solution

CF1 5EW

Dear Sir/Madam,

I am writing to complain about the inappropriate use of language and offensive remarks that I saw on your new drama programme 'The Sticks' that was broadcast last night.

Describe some background details

My family and I had been looking forward to watching this show for a number of weeks as a lot of the scenes were set in our neighbourhood and the show featured some local celebrities that we knew.

Their address

However I was appalled to see that, 5 minutes into the pilot show, there was a stream of foul language (whilst I realise that this was shown after the watershed we might have received some warning about this) and unnecessary violence. This was followed by a number of scenes which poked fun at minorities in a way which I felt was highly inappropriate.

The effect of the problems

Highlight problems of the show

Recent TV commercials had indicated that this would be a light-hearted programme appropriate for the whole family. In fact the slogan 'Where We Belong' suggested that this was a programme that would proudly showcase all the positive aspects of living in this community.

Closing statement

This opening episode left the family sad and disappointed. More importantly, it made us feel ashamed about the community we live in.

I would urge you to consider broadcasting a warning for future viewings of this show and you should also review the way you have promoted this programme.

Dear....

I look forward to hearing from you.

Your address

Yours faithfully,

Mr Windsor.

Activity 13 Put it to the proof

A member of the family has taken exception to a news item about working parents and written a letter to BBC Wales.

Review the letter. How many errors can you spot in punctuation, spelling and layout?

12 Gordon Terrace

Ebbw Vale

Mid Glamorgan

Dear to whom this may involve,

I am writing to complane about your news item about working parents neglecting children that was aired on BBC Wales last night. I felt that this portaid parents unfairly and did not explore the reasons why both parents have to find jobs in this day on age. As a working parent I would love to stay at home but I have to find work in order to make ends meat and afford the basics for my fambly.

Yours,

Ms Bennett

Test yourself

HTV Wales have asked the headteacher of your school to consider allowing them to film a new reality TV programme, charting the experiences of students and teachers over the course of a year.

Write a letter to the headteacher which argues for OR against this proposal. [20]

In your response think about:

1   using persuasive features of language;
2   setting out work appropriately for a formal letter;
3   organising your ideas appropriately in paragraphs.

Remember to complete a plan for this writing task.

Stretch

Now that you have looked at persuasive features in an article, an advertisement and a letter, choose one of the objects below (or choose an object that you have in your possession). Give yourself five minutes to write a 50–100 word 'blurb' to persuade someone else to buy it. Remember to use as many features as possible from the previous activity.

1c Growing up

Oracy

1 Disney Frozen Ice Skating Elsa: £28.99

It seems every little girl wants a piece of the *Frozen* action this festive season, and these figurine dolls are flying off the shelves.

2 Kidizoom Smart Watch: £28.99

This isn't just a watch – it takes photos and videos with fun stamps and effects, and there is also an alarm, stop watch, timer and three games.

3 Dino Zoomer Boomer Robotic T-Rex: £59.99

Boomer is a prehistoric pet for the modern age – a robotic dinosaur pet that can chase, chomp, guard and roar. His eyes change colour with his mood and there is a control pod to use.

4 Minecraft figures: £6.99

This computer game has taken children by storm, and the characters are brought to life with a selection of figures, which are only three inches tall.

5 My Friend Cayla: £42.99

This doll talks. Simply download the app to an Android or iOS smart device and connect her via Bluetooth Wireless Technology. You can ask her anything and she will answer (there are multiple safeguards in place to make her internet connection safe).

6 Bop It! Beats: £14.99

Bop It! games get you moving with fast action and unpredictability, and this one has four songs to challenge your reaction time.

Learning objectives

In this unit you will be:
- interacting in formal and informal situations;
- drawing ideas together;
- interacting with others.

Activity 1

You have decided to open up a new toy market stall in Swansea High Street for the six weeks leading up to Christmas. You will be pooling your money and resources with three other 'entrepreneurs' and you have only £2,000 to spend on stock for the first week. Choose three of the bestsellers.

To help you, we asked expert toy testers at St Joseph's RC Primary School in Gabalfa, Cardiff, to 'road-test' a selection of this year's goodies. Their verdicts are listed 1–9.

Think about:
- which products might give the biggest profit margins;
- which products you could sell most easily;
- how you would target customers.

7 Little Live Pets 2 x Love Birds & Cage: £24.99

These are interactive birds that respond to touch, and tweet, chirp and say anything you say to them.

8 Transformers Stomp & Chomp Grimlock: £55.00

This giant T-Rex figure converts from robot to dino and back in one step, and has different lights, sounds and weapons.

9 Nerf Demolisher: £26.99

The N-Strike Elite Demolisher 2-in-1 blaster from Nerf fires both Elite darts and Nerf missiles, and is recommended for children aged eight and over.

Activity 2

In groups of four, decide which toys to purchase (you can only choose up to four for the first week). How many of each would you purchase?

In your discussions, you should refer to evidence to extend your discussion, ask relevant questions and consider other people's ideas and develop your ideas fully.

Activity 3 Formal or informal?

It is important to vary your vocabulary according to the situation. Look at the market slang below and match each example up to the Standard English.

Market slang	Standard English
cakehole	a time waster
china	to look
crust	a fool, an idiot
gaff	friend, mate
gander	to have to pay for
naff	excellent
plank	cheap, tacky or poor quality
pukka	mouth
shell out	money
tyre kicker	market
wicked	authentic or 'first-rate'

Please note that it is important to vary your vocabulary as appropriate in your Individual Presentation.

Activity 4

Place these situations along the axis below. Once you have discussed this, choose **Task E** and **a less formal** context to present your ideas.

A Selling a product on the phone to a friend.

B Pitching at a stall to the public.

C Answering questions from the public about a product.

D Selling the product on a shopping channel.

E Pitching your ideas to the owner of a local market or store.

F Persuading the bank to give you an extra loan (so you can buy more stock).

Informal ◄————————————————► Formal

(my old china)   (most esteemed colleague)

Top tips

Remember to aim to use a wide range of ambitious vocabulary in your formal presentation. Also, your command of grammar has to be very strong.

Stretch

Take a lead role as the owner of Swansea market. You can only choose one group for a toy stall as there are lots of other goods that need space in your market. As different groups make their presentations, make use of probing questions to 'hire and fire', and decide on one group. To succeed in this role, you need to respond analytically to the information you receive. When giving feedback, you need to pull together all the information you have received to show complex reasoning.

Reading

Activity 5

It is important to evaluate the **reliability** of information texts. The statements below are linked to the data and research findings about parenting in Wales. Read the texts carefully and decide how reliable the statements are.

- Secondary school children are more likely to walk to school.
- Primary school children are more likely to catch a bus for longer distances.
- Secondary school children make healthier choices about how to get to school.
- Twice as many primary school children use car lifts if they live further than a mile away from school.
- The majority of parents say there are not enough suitable public places for teenagers.
- There are very few parental controls on the way teenagers use the internet.

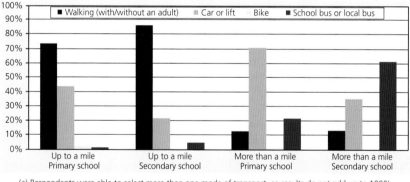

(a) Respondents were able to select more than one mode of transport, so results do not add up to 100%.

Play

54% of parents with a child aged 1 to 10 were satisfied with the play facilities in their local area; 38% with a child aged 11 to 15 were satisfied.

Of parents with a child aged 1 to 10 who were dissatisfied, 83% said there was a lack of suitable outdoor public places for their child to play and 64% said there was a lack of suitable indoor spaces.

Of parents with a child aged 11 to 15 who were dissatisfied, 77% cited a lack of suitable outdoor public places and 79% said there was a lack of indoor public places. 64% said there were too few clubs or organised activities.

http://gov.wales/docs/statistics/2015

e-Safety

Parents of children aged 7 to 15 were asked whether they used parental control filters, such as 'Net Nanny' or other filters provided by their internet service provider. 56% said that the household did use such filters, 32% had heard about them but didn't use them, and 12% had never heard of them.

Parents were also asked whether they had told their children how to stay safe online. 75% had told their child not to visit some websites; 91% not to give out personal information; 84% not to meet someone they had only met online; and 89% not to talk to strangers online.

http://gov.wales/docs/statistics/2015

Activity 6

You have been asked to take part in a debate entitled 'Are we wrapping up our children in cotton wool?' This debate will focus on how we do not encourage independence in schoolchildren in Wales.

From all the data available above, bullet-point the five most useful pieces to support your view.

Activity 7

As well as locating the reliability of evidence, the exam will also test your ability to make inferences. Read the extract from Dylan Thomas' *Portrait of the Artist as a Young Dog* (1940). What are the storyteller's feelings about Mr Samuels?

I was standing at the end of the lower playground and annoying Mr Samuels, who lived in the house just below the high railings. Mr Samuels complained once a week that boys from the school threw apples and stones and balls through his bedroom window. He sat in a deck chair in a small square of trim garden and tried to read his newspaper. I was only a few yards from him. I was staring him out. He pretended not to notice me, but I knew he knew I was standing there rudely and quietly. Every now and then he peeped at me from behind his newspaper, saw me still and serious and alone, with my eyes on his. As soon as he lost his temper I was going home. Already I was late for dinner. I had almost beaten him, the newspaper was trembling, he was breathing heavily, when a strange boy, whom I had not heard approach, pushed me down the bank.

Stretch

Incorporating the three data sources above, create a speech which argues for either:

● more parental involvement in bringing up teenagers;

● less parental involvement – encourage more freedom.

Top tips

Think about **explicit** and **implicit** meanings.

1 Questions beginning with 'What' usually ask you to **track** the text using evidence to support your ideas. However, if the evidence explains itself, there is no need to explain it. This refers to **explicit** meanings, e.g. 'the boy "disliked" him'.

2 If the evidence is **less obvious** then you will need to **explain** or **infer**, e.g. '"He snarled at him" tells us he didn't like the boy.' This refers to **implicit** meanings.

Top tips

1 This is a writer's *technique* question. Here it is important to refer to **what** is happening that makes it exciting and **how** the writer makes it more exciting and tense.

2 Try to explain **why** it is exciting and tense in your answer.

Stretch

Try to develop an extended answer to this question by explaining how tension or excitement are created.

Activity 8

Now read the rest of the story. How does the writer make the fight sound **exciting** and **tense**?

I threw a stone at his face. He took off his spectacles, put them in his coat pocket, took off his coat, hung it neatly on the railings, and attacked. Turning round as we wrestled on the top of the bank, I saw that Mr Samuels had folded his newspaper on the deck chair and was standing up to watch us. It was a mistake to turn round. The strange boy rabbit-punched me twice. Mr Samuels hopped with excitement as I fell against the railings. I was down in the dust, hot and scratched and biting, then up and dancing, and I butted the boy in the belly and we tumbled in a heap. I saw through a closing eye that his nose was bleeding. I hit his nose. He tore at my collar and spun me round by the hair.

'Come on! Come on!' I heard Mr Samuels cry.

We both turned towards him. He was shaking his fists and dodging about in the garden. He stopped then, and coughed, and set his panama straight, and avoided our eyes, and turned his back and walked slowly to the deck chair.

We both threw gravel at him.

'I'll give him "Come on!" the boy said, as we ran along the playground away from the shouts of Mr Samuels and down the steps on to the hill.

We walked home together. I admired his bloody nose. He said that my eye was like a poached egg, only black.

Sample student responses

Both the answers below are clearly focused on the question, but which one explains the best?

Student A

The writer starts with a dynamic verb 'threw' to show us that it is exciting. He also uses repetition to create tension – 'took off'.

Student B

The writer starts with the sentence 'I threw a stone at his face'. This creates tension as it seems like a very violent thing to do and we wonder if he has seriously hurt the boy.

Test yourself

Now consider the whole story. What is happening in this story? How does the reader feel about what happens? [10]

This question is asking you to display two skills.

1 The first part tests your ability to sum up **what is happening**.
2 The second part tests your ability to give a **personal response**.

Paragraph	What is happening	How do we react
I	The storyteller is trying to 'stare out' Mr Samuels	This makes us feel that the boy enjoys annoying Mr Samuels, and perhaps we feel he is being unfair.

Top tips

1 For 'What is *happening*' questions, try to sum up what is happening in each 'chunk' or paragraph of text.
2 For the personal response question, track how you feel about each of these summary points. Copy and complete the table to help you plan this.

Activity 9 Editorial skills

Order these sentences so that they make sense:
- In front of him he saw a creature with wings which looked broken and had two green eyes.
- He then realised that he needed to coax it with some food.
- The old man sat down on the bench.
- As it hopped around it seemed to stop and look at him.
- The man tried to pick it up in his hand, but each time it hopped away.

Stretch

Give one reason for your choice of the first sentence in the paragraph.

Activity 10

The following paragraph is describing the next scene when the old man finally captures the insect. This scene is to be used in a new animated film. However, the film editor has looked at it and decided that the old man is far too nice. He needs to be portrayed as an **evil villain**.

You have been asked to make five substitutions to individual words which will show his change in character.

He rummaged in his pocket and brought out a sweet that had been there a few days.

'This would do,' he thought. 'This will tempt the poor creature.'

He placed the boiled sweet within a few feet of the insect and prayed that it would do the job. The old man carefully moved his hand away and waited.

The creature suddenly hopped on the sweet. And stayed there.

The old man smiled and slowly brought his fingers closer to the insect. Pretty soon he would be able to take a closer look and look after it.

Top tips

1 You are not allowed to add any new word classes here. So a verb will have to be replaced by another verb, noun with a noun, etc.
2 Think about word associations here.
3 Verbs and nouns can be loaded with extra meaning.
4 'Hunted' is more threatening than 'rummaged'.

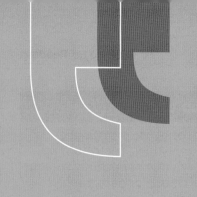

Writing

Activity 11

In pairs, think of five rules of using direct speech (you can use the examples from Activity 12 to help you).

Activity 12

Direct speech is a great way of **showing** emotions to the reader instead of **telling** the reader. Can you match up the emotion to the direct speech in the examples below:

1 'Stop lying, you miserable idiot!' the man screamed.

2 She seemed to consider for a second. 'Why don't we all cool off for a bit? There's no point everyone losing the plot. Perhaps we should …'

3 He smiled, as if he'd just thought of a joke. 'Perhaps we should give the boy a round of applause. Bravo, you genius specimen!'

4 'We must stop this right now before we all regret it,' she ordered.

5 'I d-d-didn't mean to do it. I was only trying to open it,' I stammered.

   a Sarcastic and bullying
   b Strong and determined
   c Angry and forceful
   d Helpless, lacking in confidence
   e Reasonable and sensible

Stretch

Sequence the direct speech in the right order. When you have done this, write a prequel or continue the storyline.

Activity 13 Test your accuracy

The following extract is from a story about someone doing a parachute jump for the first time. How many errors in layout and punctuation can you spot? There are about 10 errors:

'Are we going to do it' I asked.

I felt the safety harness. 'Take a deep breath, my instructor said.' I looked at him and tried to smile. 'OK.' 'When I count to ten.' he said.

'1…2…3… I started shaking 4…5…6..My mouth was dry.

Activity 14

Improve one of the following scenarios by turning it into direct speech:

The driver stopped for the hitch-hiker and offered him a lift. The hitch-hiker told the driver that he was an alien from Mars and had come down to Earth on a mission to find out as much as possible about humans. The driver said he was crazy and refused to carry on driving until he left the car but the hiker said there was no point in him trying to stop him.

Or:

I was stopped by a security guard as I left the store. He asked me to open my bag but I refused as I was with my son and I didn't want him to see the Christmas present I had bought him. The security guard didn't listen and kept on telling me to go to the office. I asked him for some proof that I had taken something but he became angry and blocked my exit. I became really angry and embarrassed.

Varying your sentence structure

It is important to vary sentences in order to make your writing more interesting. The box below shows six ways of varying sentences:

• '-ing' starters (present participle): *Walking down the street, I caught the eye of an old friend.*	• Minor sentences (sentences without a subject or verb): *More bad luck. The story of my life.*
• '-ly' starter (adverb): **Slowly**, *I turned the corner.*	• Exclamatives: *Phew! The ordeal was over!*
• Conjunction starters: **As** *she looked up, she saw …* **After** *running for five hours, he gave up.* A sentence which starts with a subordinate conjunction will make a *complex sentence*.	• Questions: *Why was I always last?*

Activity 15

The following passage needs a wider variety of sentence structures. Can you improve this by including different sentence structures:

I was sitting on the sofa watching the numbers come up and the man showed numbers 24 and 42. I was getting excited at this point and my heart skipped a beat when 6 came out as this was on my ticket too. The man then said the numbers 18 and 50. I was already imagining being on a yacht in the Bahamas enjoying a cocktail. The man on the telly seemed to be looking me in the eye and he pulled out the last number. I suddenly couldn't believe my eyes when he picked out the final ball.

Stretch

Continue the writing above by using a wide variety of sentences. Can you incorporate direct speech?

Activity 16 Narrative writing

Although there is no set pattern or set of rules for writing a good story, there are usually four main elements of a story:

Setting	Crisis
Usually introduces time, place, character, and atmosphere.	This is when the problem builds into crisis point.
This is where you can show your descriptive skills.	You need to think about sentence varieties and sharp use of direct speech.
Hook	**Resolution**
This can be a problem, a dare, a sudden appearance, a mission or a challenge.	This is how you resolve the story. Does it end well or badly?
You might want to include some direct speech to move your narrative on.	Think about ending your story with a message or moral.

Can you spot the elements of the story below?

Her father kept teasing her.

'Football is a boy's game. No one's interested in girls' football.'

'You're just a sexist pig! You belong in the dark ages!'

'I bet you wouldn't last twenty minutes in my team.'

It was a cold morning on Mary Avenue as Shelby stepped onto the pitch. The ground was rock hard.

Two days later she couldn't believe it. She was still beaming. She couldn't help laughing when she heard her father tell her Nan that he was never so unhappy to see his team score a winning goal.

Suddenly she felt a searing pain in her ankle. As she was about to strike for goal, a defender had sliced into her.

'Are you OK, Shels?' her team-mate asked.

'No – but I'm not giving in now!' There was no way she was going to lose this bet.

Activity 17 Final advice for narrative writing

Separate the advice below into the columns of the table.

Essential advice	Think about	Avoid

Stretch

Fill in 'the gaps' in the story at the bottom of page 32. How might you develop each of these sections?

- Keep to the past tense
- Only have up to three characters in a story
- Let your imagination run wild
- Use paragraphs
- Use the first person
- Keep to the same tense throughout
- Include lots of different characters
- Stretch your story over a number of days
- Make your story realistic
- Use exotic locations for your narrative
- Always write in a specific genre
- Simple storylines work well
- Try to include a twist in the story
- Take care with spelling, punctuation and grammar
- Vary your sentences and vocabulary
- Use slang
- Actions and direct speech are more interesting to read than description
- Hook the reader by starting at the crisis point then 'flashback' to the setting
- Keep your story to a tight timeline – no more than one or two days

---

Test yourself

Choose one of these titles for your narrative:

Write about a time when you felt that you were treated unfairly.

Or

Write an account of a time when you – or someone else – did something special. [35]

Remember to produce a plan for your narrative and try to follow the essential advice from Activity 17. For the second task, you can use the first or third person.

Unit 2: Leisure

2a   A sporting chance

Oracy

Learning objectives

In this unit you will be:

- interacting with others;
- responding to questions and ideas;
- drawing ideas together.

Activity 1

The NHS recommends that young people should do at least 60 minutes of physical activity every day and greatly reduce the time spent sitting down.

Your school has read this recommendation and would like to offer an extra two hours of exercise per week. The headteacher has researched local sports clubs and narrowed the choice down to four options. The school has to choose one of these to be their new sport initiative.

Look at the extracts below and decide which sport would most appeal to students and parents.

Think about:

- the benefits of taking up each sport;
- any disadvantages that each sport presents.

Karate

Vale Karate really is Karate for everyone. We aim to make each student's time with Vale Karate, be it a week or two, or a lifetime, enjoyable and beneficial. Karate is:

- a place to meet old friends and make new ones;
- a place to improve your fitness and wellbeing, reduce stress and take advantage of the wide array of benefits Karate delivers, both physically and mentally;
- a place to learn the absorbing and challenging art of Shotokan and the exciting sport of Karate.

Karate is more than simply a sport and we aim to ensure that training with Vale Karate is an extremely positive experience for absolutely anyone.

Cost per student: £5   Length of class: 1 hour

Size of group: 30   Travelling time from school: 15 minutes

www.valekarate.com

Windsurfing

With different board and sail sizes, windsurfing can be tailored to children easily. Windsurfing uses bodyweight, not big muscles, to work the sail and the challenge is more mental than muscular. That said, an hour or two afloat can provide as good a workout as the gym. Inland, you can learn to windsurf at one of the many lakes all over the UK. After two days, you'll know sailing theory and will have mastered sailing to a point and back. You'll also have lots of fun.

Cost per student: £7

Size of group: 15

Length of class: 1 hour (+ 15 minutes preparation)

Travelling time from school: 30 minutes

www.visitwales.com

Outdoor circuits

'Nicky Palmer Fitness' offers outdoor fitness for everyone. Get ready to go back to basics … no flat screen television, no mirrors, no spending half the session on your phone like people do at the gym – just exercises that are designed to help you tone up and get in shape. Traditionally, such sessions have been referred to as 'bootcamps'. The phrase tends to evoke thoughts of drill sergeants barking orders and yelling. That's not us. Our sessions are designed to suit your fitness needs and abilities. With the encouragement of your fitness instructor, the sessions are designed to cater for all fitness levels, age, gender and abilities. Everyone is constantly encouraging one another, which provides motivation to inspire and encourage progression.

Cost per student: £6

Size of group: 32

Length of class: 1 hour

Travelling time from school: 5 minutes

www.nickypalmerfitness.co.uk

Swimming

The International Pool improvement programme offers lessons for both children and adults on a group basis. Swimming is a life skill which everyone should have the opportunity to master in their lifetime. We are dedicated to ensuring that, whatever their age or ability, everyone can have fun while learning to swim! With that in mind, our swimming lesson programme is designed to suit all ages and abilities. It is endorsed by the Amateur Swimming Association which ensures that our teachers are fully qualified and inspiring. Swimming is an important life skill. Contact us today to learn how we can help you swim well!

Cost per student: £4.90

Size of group: 10

Length of class: 30 minutes

Travelling time from school: 15 minutes

www.leisurecentre.com

> ### Stretch
> Identify the persuasive techniques used in each text. Try to explain how these techniques persuade the reader.

Activity 2

In groups of four, take the roles below to ensure that the headteacher chooses the most suitable sport for your school. As a group, you will need to make a final decision on one of the sports given.

You are a headteacher	You are a pupil from the school council
Think about the benefits: ● improved fitness ● new opportunities ● reputation of the school. Consider any concerns: ● the cost to the school ● health and safety issues ● popularity of the sport with students.	Think about the benefits: ● improved fitness ● new opportunities ● variety in the school day. Consider any concerns: ● health and safety issues ● whether students would enjoy it.
You are a parent	**You are a PE teacher**
Think about the benefits: ● improved fitness ● new opportunities. Consider any concerns: ● health and safety issues ● whether it would take up study time ● whether your own child would enjoy it.	Think about the benefits: ● improved fitness ● new opportunities. Consider any concerns: ● travelling to venues when there are sporting facilities on site ● whether traditional school sports would lose out.

Stretch

Before the final group decision is presented, make a list of 'argument-building' words and phrases that can be used to qualify your choice more clearly.

For example:

Our first concern was whether … We also had to appraise … When reviewing the information … Moreover … Notwithstanding …

Activity 3 Summing up

When you have completed the group discussion, present your decision to the class with the reasons for your choice.

Reading

Learning objectives

In this unit you will be:
- exploring the difference between continuous and non-continuous texts;
- distinguishing between statements which are and are not supported;
- evaluating ideas and character in texts.

Activity 4 Continuous or non-continuous text?

You need to understand these key terms in order to attempt this task:
- **Continuous text** – texts in which sentences are usually organised into paragraphs or sections, for example, in narratives, articles or letters. These paragraphs or sections are often linked in time order or order of ideas.
- **Non-continuous text** – information and meaning can be taken from different parts of a non-continuous text. You may need to 'jump around' the page to read it. Websites, tables, schedules, graphs and infographics are usually organised like this.

Look at the texts below. Identify whether each text is continuous or non-continuous.

Text type	Continuous	Non-continuous
A Diary		
B Short story		
C Map		
D Graph		
E Formal letter		

Text A: Diary: 'The Diary of Samuel Pepys, 1660'

August 28th

I went to bed a little troubled as I fear my boy Will is a thief and has stolen some money of mine – particularly a letter that Mr Jenkins left with me last week with half a crown in to send to his son.

August 29th

Before I went to the office, my wife and I talked to my boy Will about his stealing of things but he denied all with the greatest subtlety and confidence in the world.

Text B: Short story extract: opening from 'Numerology' by Christian Michener (New Rivers Press/October 2006)

The girl Ryan Callaway was following turned off the Boulevard St. Michel, where Ryan knew every shop and office, and onto a side street that he hadn't been on before, even though he had been wandering the city streets for weeks. She walked past a papeterie and an abandoned shoe store and an art gallery selling glossy prints of American movie posters and then led the way into a dimly lit office that once might have been used by an insurance salesman. To Ryan the room smelled like his parents' basement back in the States, a wet and musty resting place for the broken appliances and old clothes the family couldn't bring themselves to part with.

Text C: Map: Folly Farm, Pembrokeshire

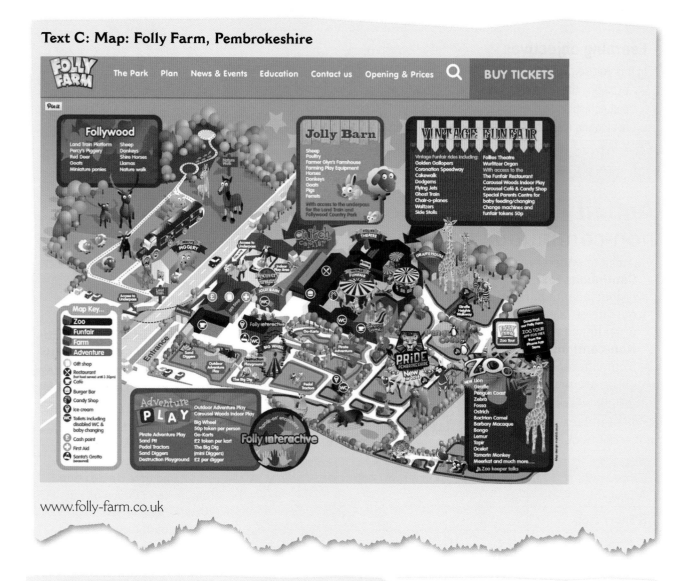

www.folly-farm.co.uk

Text D: Scatter graph

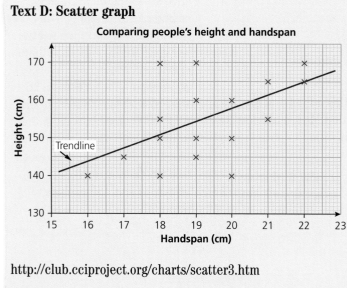

Comparing people's height and handspan

http://club.cciproject.org/charts/scatter3.htm

Text E: Formal letter

Dear Sir,

I must express my dissatisfaction regarding a holiday that I recently took with your company. I travelled to Buenos Aires for a holiday from 16 to 23 April.

My first issue is with the rude manner of your airport ground staff.

Stretch

Think of three examples of your own continuous and non-continuous texts.

Activity 5

When you are reading a text that establishes a point of view about a topic, ask yourself if the points and claims are supported with reasons or evidence.

Read the following texts and decide if the points made are supported or unsupported.

1   It's all very well saying kids don't exercise as much now as they did back in the 1950s but it doesn't recognise that life has changed. Without computers, video games and mobiles, children played outside much more back then. Technology is distracting us from physical activity.

2   There isn't time in a modern school curriculum for as much PE as there used to be. We've got more subjects to study now that didn't even exist 70 years ago. I would say that, because of this, there's more pressure on children now than ever before.

3   It's almost impossible to eat a healthy diet after a day at school or work.

4   We're becoming increasingly overweight as a nation.

5   Walking round the supermarket or the shops isn't going to be enough to keep you fit and healthy. The government suggests that adults do about 30 minutes of activity five days a week.

Stretch

Look at the examples that you have decided have unsupported points. Add another sentence to these – including your own evidence – so that they **are** supported.

Activity 6

Read the following texts and answer the questions that follow.

Text A: Encouraging Your Child to be Physically Active

How can I get my child to be more physically active?

With participation in all types of physical activity declining dramatically as a child's age and grade in school increases, it is important that physical activity be a regular part of family life. Studies have shown that lifestyles learned as children are much more likely to stay with a person into adulthood. It is a problem if sports and physical activities are not a family priority, as children will not see the value of regular exercise.

Did you know?

•   Studies show that children spend nearly three hours a day watching TV.

•   Only half of children and teens, ages 12 to 21, exercise regularly.

•   Children who do not exercise have more chance of becoming overweight.

•   Overweight teens have a 70% chance of becoming overweight adults.

www.healthychildren.org

Text B: I've never had a better week

My post on Monday mentioned that it's been difficult to avoid the between-meal food. I'm happy to report that it hasn't been a problem this week! I'm eating more at meals, and I'm also making sure to take a healthy snack for the afternoon. I eat fruit. I avoid carbs but I increased protein. I stopped drinking lemonade. I believe that not eating enough at meals and drinking sugary drinks were the two biggest reasons I cheated during the day with chocolate.

In my last update post, I also said that I would tweet my workouts. I have been struggling to find the time to fit exercise in after work, but I'm going to write myself a note to remember to do it. I owe myself a run today. I would appreciate it if followers could remind me on days that I don't tweet my workout. It helps me.

Call to action!

I'd love it if you did this challenge with me. Check out the challenge article at Upgrade Reality and sign up. Then tell me about it, and we will do this together!

www.findingmyfitness.com

Text C: PE-letter mum: family reveal what happened next after sport-hating girl handed sick note to teacher

By Lauren Brown, Sam Webb

Olivia McEvoy, 11, made a bid to get out of sports lessons that backfired badly when she asked her mum to write a note excusing her.

A schoolgirl who tried to bunk off PE saw her cunning plan backfire when her mother mischievously packed her off to classes with a sicknote admitting she had 'Bone-idle-itus'.

Little Olivia McEvoy, 11, would repeatedly beg her mum, Sam, to write her a note saying that she was too poorly in a bid to get her out of the lesson.

Eventually Mrs McEvoy was so fed up of Olivia's pestering, she gave her daughter the sealed note and asked to give it to the headmaster and even agreed she did not need to take her kit with her to school.

But unbeknown to Olivia, mother-of-two Sam, 27, had in fact written a very truthful but tongue-in-cheek note to staff which revealed the schoolgirl's plan in full. It read,

'Olivia has requested that I write her a note for PE. Here it is ... Olivia is perfectly fit and well to take part in her PE lesson today. The only thing she's suffering with is a severe case of Bone-idle-itus. Olivia's complaint is, it's too cold to participate. Might I suggest a few extra laps to warm her up? Please return to Olivia after reading.'

Olivia then discovered her PE kit had already been dropped off at reception. Needless to say, Olivia did take part in the lesson and even scored three goals in football. Her mum said: 'Unfortunately she didn't have to do the extra laps but she actually really enjoyed PE and had a good lesson. However, she didn't speak to me at all that night.

'There's no chance she'll be doing it again in a hurry. It's a lesson to her that she can't get out of things she doesn't like.'

www.mirror.co.uk

For Text A:

1 Identify two health risks of not exercising.

For Text B:

2 Explain why the blogger no longer needs to eat chocolate during the day.

For Text C:

3 **Organise** the content of the article into the correct sequence:
   a Olivia's PE kit had been dropped off at school.
   b Mrs McEvoy was fed up of her daughter's attitude.
   c Olivia refused to speak to her mother.
   d The note revealed Olivia's plan.

4 Paragraph four tells us that the contents of the letter were 'unbeknown' to Olivia. Choose a word or phrase from the list below that best defines 'unbeknown'.
   a encouraged
   b to find out later
   c without knowledge
   d hidden.

Test yourself

How do you feel about Mrs McEvoy's actions in the report? In your answer focus on what she *says* and *does*. [10]

This table is useful for organising your answer:

What Mrs McEvoy says and does	How we react to these
She puts a letter in the bag.	*'I think that …'*
She lets her daughter go to school with no kit.	

Evaluating character in texts

The exam might include a question where you have to evaluate a character in a text. This question might begin with 'How do you feel about...' or 'What do you think...' and might address you as a reader.

Top tips

Even though the Test yourself question begins with 'How …', it is not asking you, on <u>this</u> occasion, to look at the writer's technique. As the question is aimed directly at 'you' then we know that this is testing your ability to **evaluate** her actions. Better answers will avoid simple opinions and will support ideas with the text.

Stretch

Use any of the prompts below to come up with a new question for each of Texts A, B and C. Which are the best prompts to test the following skills: analysis, location, inference, synthesis:

● How many?
● In what ways?
● How does the writer show …?
● Explain why …
● What do you learn about …?
● What is the writer's attitude to …?

Writing

Learning objectives

In this unit you will be:
- adapting your style to suit task and purpose – advertisement writing;
- paragraphing and presenting work appropriately;
- developing persuasive writing.

Activity 7

Read the following article and complete the activity that follows.

From Big Man to Iron Man

He was unable to swim the length of a swimming pool but Chris Thomas is now hoping to complete an Ironman challenge after losing more than eight stone.

The 43-year-old will be swimming, cycling and running his way to achieving his goal following his dramatic weight loss from more than 22st to 14st.

Chris, from Barry, frequently ate takeaways and didn't exercise which caused him to put on weight, and he found it difficult to walk up a flight of stairs or ride his bike.

He said, 'I'd always tried diets and always had the best intentions of losing weight. I never thought of myself as someone who was fat. I saw myself every day in the mirror and it has just happened over time.'

The weight dropped off

While reading a newspaper, Chris came across an advert for Nicky Palmer fitness sessions in Barry, which he decided to attend in another attempt to ditch the weight.

The council IT specialist said, 'I sent Nicky a text and I went along but didn't tell anyone because I thought it would be a train wreck. I ended up really enjoying it and went to all the sessions and the weight dropped off. It was all through exercise, eating sensibly and keeping measurements. I lost just under eight stone!'

Loads more energy

After the weight loss, Chris attended a session where Nicky made him wear a rucksack with weights inside.

It wasn't until after the session that Nicky told Chris he was carrying the amount of weight he had lost!

Now Chris is taking on the gruelling Ironman Challenge, which takes place on North Beach in Tenby, after being signed up by Nicky. The challenge consists of a 2.4 mile swim, a 112 mile bike ride and a 26.2 mile run.

He said, 'I couldn't swim half a length of the swimming pool when I started training and I was gasping for air. I joined the Cardiff Triathletes, and with their help the swimming has become the strongest of the three disciplines. At the moment, I am feeling a little bit tired and the training is getting me down a bit. When it's over and done with, I don't know what I'm going to do!'

Chris shares his routine

BEFORE: I would skip breakfast. For lunch, I would eat sandwiches, pasties and a bag of crisps.

For evening meals, I would eat takeaways, including pizza, chips and Chinese meals. Throughout the day, I would drink two litres of fizzy pop.

AFTER: Now I eat fresh fruit for breakfast. For lunch, I have a ham salad sandwich, as well as protein porridge. For evening meals, I'll eat some quiche with vegetables.

EXERCISE: I attend three fitness sessions a week, involving lifting tyres, press-ups, sit-ups and running.

www.walesonline.co.uk

Look again at the article. In the table below, give an example of each technique you find.

Feature	Definition	Example from the article
Strong, emotive language		*'gruelling,' 'gasping for air'*
	Facts and figures	
Expert opinion/ professional advice		
		'swimming, cycling and running'
	Stories from personal life	
Use of images and pictures		

Stretch

Insert three more appropriate subheadings in the article. Try to use alliteration, rhyme or a pun/play on words.

For example, the paragraph 7 subheading could rhyme – 'Lifted what he shifted'.

Activity 8 Put it to the proof

Find all the errors in this advertisement on the internet.

AMAZING CHANSE!

By one get one free daytime or nightime. The best offer on the web just got better with are amazing wait loss programme. Just supscribe now by filling in your Name and addres below and you will recieve two month's off our increable weight loss meals for the price of one. Hundreds of cutomers cant be wrong. Sing up now many savings for you.

What errors did you spot? Identify these as Spelling, Punctuation or Grammar errors and put in a table like the one below.

Spelling	Punctuation	Grammar
e.g. supscribe	e.g. no full stops	e.g. expression errors

Test yourself

Imagine that you run a local fitness group. You decide to produce a new advertisement, promoting the fitness sessions. It is up to you to decide what sort of physical activity or sport these sessions involve. [20]

Ideas:

indoor or outdoor circuits with exercise 'stations' of a different exercise at each stop

aerobics   Zumba (aerobic dancing)   yoga

spinning (cycling an exercise bike)   weights

Alternatively, you can choose a particular sport that you know about. For example:

gymnastics   martial arts   swimming

trampolining   athletics

You could even make up a new class. For example:

Turbo kick   Body Blast   Abs Zone   Aerobic Energy

Planning your answer

As advertisements have to be eye-catching and organised, think of some catchy subheadings for each of the topic sentences below:

- The advantages of attending the fitness sessions.
- An explanation of what goes on at the sessions.
- Testimonials (recommendations) from people who have attended and improved their fitness.
- Reassurance for those who may be concerned about coming along.
- Details of times and prices.
- Any other information that you think is relevant.

Remember to:

- Use headings and subheadings to organise the information.
- Vary your sentence structures. You could start with a statement, 'It is likely that …', a personal pronoun, 'You might think that …', 'We welcome …', an interrogative pronoun, 'When …', 'What …', or an adverb, 'Surprisingly …', 'Usually …'.
- Paragraph your work appropriately. Remember that a slightly new focus or topic needs a new paragraph.
- Include language features appropriate for persuasive writing:

  Positive emotive words   Statistics

  Tripling or listing   Expert opinion/professional advice

  Informal words   Exaggeration

While the language features above may add to the quality of the writing, it is important to realise that they are not a 'formula for success'. Any such features should not be forced, but used naturally in your expression or written 'voice', where appropriate.

Self-assessment

When your advertising leaflet is finished, complete the grid below with examples of the techniques that you have used.

Features to use	Have I used them? (Yes/No)
I have used headings and subheadings to organise information.	
I have varied my sentences.	
My work has been appropriately paragraphed.	
I have used some persuasive language techniques.	
I have proofread my work for errors.	

Sample student response

This is the opening of a leaflet advertising a karate session.

Have you ever tried a martial art? Well, come on down to Princetown Shotokan Karate Club and give it a go!

Here at Princetown, we welcome beginners of all ages and abilities. You don't need to have tried a martial art before to come along. We meet every Monday, Wednesday and Friday from 6-7 at Princetown Leisure Centre. The cost is only £4 a session or you can pay for a block of ten classes for only £35, saving you £10.

Identify any features from the list above. What are the areas for improvement?

Oracy

Learning objectives

In this unit you will be:
- interacting with others;
- responding to questions and ideas;
- drawing ideas together.

Activity 1

Rank order the following destinations from 'most likely' to 'least likely' to visit.

Think about:
- what you can see and do at each destination;
- any drawbacks to any of the destinations.

Text A: Orlando, Florida

Orlando is the undisputed theme park capital of the world! More than 50,000 acres of turf in the region are covered by amusement parks, and the lion's share is owned by famous names like Universal and Disney. There are more rollercoasters out here than there are days in the month. On the whitest knuckle rides you get launched from 0 to 40 miles per hour in 2 seconds and become inverted 5 times at 50 miles-per-hour. There's plenty for families, too – killer whale shows and tours of Cinderella's castle are just the start of the story.

(Thomson holiday brochure)

www.thomson.co.uk

Text B: Queenstown, New Zealand

Queenstown, New Zealand, is the Southern Hemisphere's premier four season lake and alpine resort. Queenstown's stunning scenery, huge range of activities and renowned warm welcome cement its reputation as New Zealand's favourite visitor destination. Surrounded by majestic mountains and set on the shores of crystal clear Lake Wakatipu, the natural beauty and the unique energy of the region create the perfect backdrop for a holiday full of adventure, exploration or relaxation.

(Queenstown, New Zealand, official website)

www.queenstownnz.co.nz

Text C: Sydney, Australia

Live the Australian dream in the sun-drenched city of Sydney. Surf the waves, climb the Harbour Bridge, have lunch at The Rocks, study the iconic shapes of the Sydney Opera House, and then tour the world with an array of extraordinary cuisine. All this awaits you on holidays in Sydney.

Home to some of the world's most recognisable landmarks, Sydney is the perfect place for those who love to combine buzzing city life with the great outdoors.

(TravelSupermarket.com website)

www.travelsupermarket.com

Text D: Hong Kong, China

Hong Kong is known for its fascinating harmony between old and new, east and west. With 5,000 years of Chinese traditions, this is a truly unique city. For beaches, traditional markets and laid back cafés, head to the island's south coast. For serious shoppers there is no rival to the vast malls and stalls that line the streets on the Kowloon Peninsula. Explore the streets of Tsim Sha Tsui, famous for sprawling shopping complexes and street traders hawking their wares. To experience a taste of rural life, visit the New Territories where mountainous country parks are interspersed with ancient temples.

(Kuoni holiday brochure)

www.kuoni.co.uk/hong-kong

Text E: Koh Samui, Thailand

Koh Samui is an island paradise off the east coast of Thailand and faces onto the waters of the Gulf of Siam. Holidays here offer something for party-goers, as well as those who want to rest and relax or enjoy some of the many spa treatments on offer. There are plenty of things to see and do while in Koh Samui; you just have to raise yourself from that sun lounger for a few hours and explore! The Golden Buddha at Wat Phra Yai is striking and the Na Muang waterfalls are a sight to behold. Let your cares float away as you relax on Koh Samui's beaches. If you get restless, Fisherman's Village with its boutiques and restaurants is a great place to while away an afternoon.

(TravelSupermarket.com website)

www.travelsupermarket.com

Activity 2

A family of four have decided to book the holiday of a lifetime. However, with each family member being of a different age with different interests, settling on a choice is difficult. In groups of four, take on one of the roles outlined in the boxes below and try to come to a decision about your top three choices.

You are the **48-year-old father**. Your interests are water sports and trying new, extreme sports. You like the great outdoors and the chance to try something new on a holiday. You dislike theme parks and over-commercialised places.	You are the **45-year-old mother**. Your interests are shopping, hiking and eating out. You would like to go somewhere exciting but also want the chance to relax and unwind. You dislike package holidays where you are stuck in the same place.
You are the **15-year-old son**. Your interests are skateboarding and theme parks. You dislike sunbathing and secluded places with nothing to do.	You are the **10-year-old daughter**. You enjoy swimming and playing on the beach. You dislike sunbathing and trying new foods.

Activity 3

When you have completed the family discussion, present your decision to the class with reasons for your choice.

> *Stretch*
>
> The words below are useful for presenting your ideas using more sophisticated vocabulary:
> - considered
> - deliberated
> - reflected
> - acknowledged
> - contemplated
> - recognised.
>
> Turn these words into abstract nouns. For example, *considered* becomes *consideration*. Try to incorporate these words into your presentation.

Reading

Learning objectives

In this unit you will be:

- exploring form, purpose and audience;
- retrieving information;
- analysing the writer's technique.

Text A

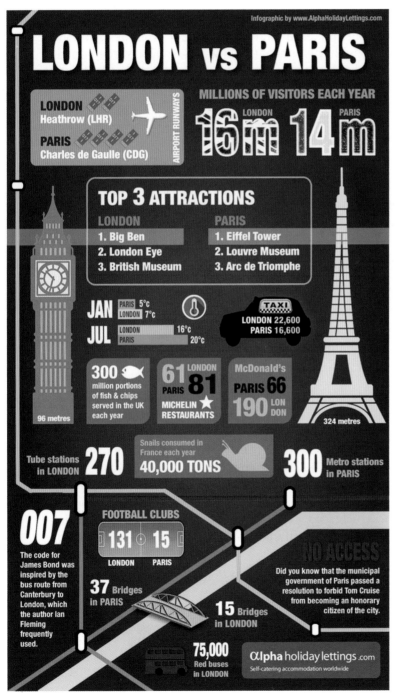

Infographic by www.AlphaHolidayLettings.com

LONDON vs PARIS

LONDON Heathrow (LHR)
PARIS Charles de Gaulle (CDG)

AIRPORT RUNWAYS

MILLIONS OF VISITORS EACH YEAR

LONDON **16 m**   PARIS **14 m**

TOP 3 ATTRACTIONS

LONDON	PARIS
1. Big Ben	1. Eiffel Tower
2. London Eye	2. Louvre Museum
3. British Museum	3. Arc de Triomphe

JAN PARIS 5°c / LONDON 7°c
JUL LONDON 16°c / PARIS 20°c

TAXI LONDON 22,600 / PARIS 16,600

300 million portions of fish & chips served in the UK each year

61 LONDON **81** PARIS MICHELIN RESTAURANTS

McDonald's PARIS **66** **190** LONDON

96 metres

324 metres

Tube stations in LONDON **270**

Snails consumed in France each year **40,000 TONS**

300 Metro stations in PARIS

007 The code for James Bond was inspired by the bus route from Canterbury to London, which the author Ian Fleming frequently used.

FOOTBALL CLUBS **131** LONDON **15** PARIS

37 Bridges in PARIS

15 Bridges in LONDON

NO ACCESS Did you know that the municipal government of Paris passed a resolution to forbid Tom Cruise from becoming an honorary citizen of the city.

75,000 Red buses in LONDON

αlpha holiday lettings .com
Self-catering accommodation worldwide

www.alphaholidaylettings.com

Activity 4

An infographic is an informative, visual way of presenting information.

Look at Text A, the infographic to the left, and answer the questions that follow.

1 Which destination is more popular with tourists?

2 How many underground stations are there in total in London and Paris?

3 Which of the two cities are generally warmer in summer?

4 What statistic does not have a comparison?

5 What are the names of the two airports, and which has the most landing strips?

Text B: from *Tower: An Epic History of the Tower of London*, Nigel Jones (Random House publishing, 2012)

No building has been more intimately involved in the story of Britain than the Tower of London – a mighty, brooding stronghold in the very heart of the capital. Castle, prison, torture chamber, execution site, zoo, mint, treasure house, armoury, observatory: the Tower has been all these things and more, standing at the epicentre of dramatic, bloody and frequently cruel events for almost a thousand years.

Activity 5

Text A, 'London vs Paris,' is in the form of an infographic in order to present facts about the cities in a visual way. It is aimed at tourists. The presentation might appeal to younger adults whose familiarity with the internet means that they are more used to reading graphic, non-continuous texts. Look at the texts opposite and below and complete the table on the next page. Text A has been completed.

Text C: Regular travellers/commuters

If you travel regularly or commute around London, a season ticket will usually provide the best deal for you. Annual season tickets generally provide the best value as you will get about a year's travel for the price of 10 months'. If you make the same journey more than three or four times a week, on most routes, season tickets will be the best value for money.

www.londontravelwatch.org.uk

Text D: 'Fantastic visit to this stunning hotel'
Reviewed 21 June 2015

This is a beautiful 5* hotel in the centre of London (just opposite Marylebone tube station which means it's brilliant for accessing the centre of the city). First impressions are great, with a lovely 1930s décor and it's very well maintained. The room we had was spacious and very clean; the bed was large and comfortable and the bathroom was huge. The atrium where they serve dinner/breakfast is a stunning environment and we had a quick visit to the mirror bar for one of the best cocktails I've had for a while. The biggest factor was the friendliness of the staff who couldn't do enough for you.

www.tripadvisor.co.uk

Text	Form	Purpose	Audience	Explanation (how you identified the audience)
A	Infographic	Informs/gives facts about London and Paris	Tourists, young people – teenagers, young adults	Dynamic, bright presentation; non-continuous text would appeal to younger people
B				
C				
D				

Activity 6

The following article from *The Daily Mail* is about the information shown in the infographic that you have looked at in Activity 4.
Read the article and answer the questions that follow.

Text A: London vs Paris: The infographic that puts the two capitals head-to-head in their battle for supremacy, by Sarah Gordon

They are two cities that always seem to be in competition – especially when it comes to which is the most popular with tourists.

Now one company has compared the highlights of London and Paris to see which capital city comes out on top.

While London seemingly boasts more visitors, the French capital certainly beats us on cuisine - with 81 Michelin-star restaurants and just 66 branches of McDonald's, compared to 61 Michelin-star restaurants in London and 190 branches of the fast-food outlet.

However, footballers will be much happier in London, with 131 clubs to choose from if they want to watch a match – of varying different professional levels – while Paris has just 15 across the city.

While comparing attractions and sights is certainly interesting, the latest infographic comparing Paris and London is certainly set to spark rows over the all-important visitor numbers.

When Office of National Statistics figures showed a huge increase in visitors to London, prompting questions about whether the capital was about to de-throne Paris as the most visited city in the world, the French capital hit back declaring London just 'a suburb of Paris'.

London Mayor, Boris Johnson, said: 'These incredible figures prove that London is, without doubt, the greatest city on the planet. With so many fascinating museums, the best theatre scene in the world, more green space than any other European city, numerous top sporting venues, a low crime rate and much else besides, it's no wonder that people from all over the globe are flocking to London in record numbers.'

Tom Lei from AlphaHolidayLettings.com, who put together the infographic, said, 'It is definitely a contentious issue when it comes to which city is better or attracts more visitors. The Diamond Jubilee and Olympic Games in 2012 showcased London to the world and we will see the positive impact in terms of people wanting to visit the city for years to come.'

www.dailymail.co.uk

Top tips

When answering a multiple choice question:

1 Make sure that you have read it carefully as part of the whole sentence or paragraph.

2 Try to anticipate the correct response by covering the options.

3 If you find the response that you expected, circle it but double-check that none of the other responses are better.

1 **Organise** the content of the article into the correct sequence:
   a The Mayor considers London the greatest city on the planet.
   b Big national events have drawn attention to London.
   c London and Paris always seem to be in competition.
   d There has been a huge increase in visitors to London.

2 Explain the following phrases in your own words:
   a 'seemingly boasts more visitors'
   b London is just "'a suburb of Paris"'.

3 Identify **one** fact and **one** opinion that present London as 'better' than Paris.

4 Paragraph six tells us that Paris 'hit back' at suggestions that London was better. Choose a word or phrase from the list below that could be used instead of 'hit back'.

   ... the French capital _____ declaring London just 'a suburb of Paris'.

   a noticed
   b criticised this
   c retreated
   d recoiled

5 Find two examples of positive language that the Mayor uses in paragraph seven to make London sound great. What is the effect of these words?

6 In the final paragraph, Tom Lei calls the issue of which city is the better 'contentious'. **Select** one definition from the list below that best defines this word:
   a to have huge differences
   b interesting
   c likely to cause an argument
   d doubtful.

Stretch

The Daily Mail text is a good example of journalese. Two typical features of this type of writing include dynamic verbs that are slightly informal – 'the French capital hit back' – and hyperbole (exaggerations) – 'greatest city'. Identify as many examples of these features as possible and discuss the effect on the reader.

Activity 7

Read the following extract.

Compared to other cities, such as Sydney or Tokyo, the centre of London is relatively _____(1)_____ and can be negotiated quite easily. The Underground train system serves _____(2)_____ stations and enables visitors to _____(3)_____ the city without difficulty. At under £7 for a day's Pay as you go Oyster card in central London, the price is _____(4)_____ for most people.

Choose the word which best fits the gap:

1	unusual	compact	bizarre	empty
2	numerous	congested	scarce	neat
3	enter	leave	traverse	search
4	cheap	extortionate	luxurious	affordable

Activity 8

Read the following text which aims to attract visitors to The London Dungeon tourist attraction, then answer this question:

How does the writer create fear and excitement in The London Dungeon text? [10]

Comment on:

- what visitors will experience in The London Dungeon;
- the words and phrases that create fear and excitement.

WHAT IS THE DUNGEON?

We are a thrill-filled journey through London's dark past. You get 110 minutes of laughs, scares, theatre, shocks, rides, special effects, characters, jokes and storytelling. The recommended age for The London Dungeon is twelve years and above, however, it is up to the discretion of the accompanying adult. Many children enter The London Dungeon and enjoy the experience, but please be aware that it does get very dark inside the building and there are some loud noises.

So, are you ready?

Descend into the heart of the Dungeon in the medieval lift. Hear the grinding cogs and chains as the winches strain. Don't worry, it hardly ever falls …

Meet the Lift Jester

Join our resident Lift Jester as you descend. This cheerful fellow will prepare you for a thousand years of gloriously horrible history. It all starts here! What's that? You hear the sounds of water lapping against the shore? With luck, you have arrived safely at Thames river docks.

What you'll learn

- Whether the lift actually works.
- If the Jester's jokes are remotely funny...
- Who's the most scared (and likely to be picked on!).

Source: www.thedungeons.com

Top tips

Remember, as explained in Unit 1, questions beginning with:

How does the writer …

How does the text …

are asking you to comment on the writer's **technique**. Before answering, identify the focus words (in this case '**fear**' and '**excitement**').

1 Focus on 'fear' and 'excitement'.
2 Refer to a range of evidence.
3 Explain HOW the evidence tries to create fear/excitement.

Sample student responses

Which one of these sample answers addresses the task most effectively? What advice would you give Student A to improve their response?

Student A

The writer makes The London Dungeon sound frightening by using lots of great words like 'shocks' and 'loud noises'. These are really effective.

Student B

The London Dungeon is made to sound frightening in a variety of ways. It is described as 'thrill-filled' which makes it sound like it will be really good fun. The words 'scares' and 'shocks' add to this by suggesting that you will be scared but 'laughs' and 'jokes' suggest that it will be enjoyable rather than terrifying.

Student C

The word 'Dungeon' already conjures up ideas of a frightening place. We are told that you should be over 12 to go in but an accompanying adult needs to decide which suggests that children could be scared in this place. The Dungeon is 'very dark' with 'loud noises'. These phrases create a frightening atmosphere.

Writing

Learning objectives

In this unit you will be:

- developing proofreading skills;
- adapting your style to suit form and purpose;
- developing argumentation writing;
- adapting register to suit your audience.

Activity 9

You have found a website that appears to be offering cheap entry tickets to London's tourist attractions. Find the mistakes in the text that show you that this is not a genuine offer but a fake site designed to trick people.

> **BEST PRICE GURANTEED!**
>
> Enjoy London with special London vocher for entry to main atractions. This voucher is special voucher as you pay one combined price show your Voucher at entry for over 20 top attractions. This Great deal makes is easyer for you and you're family to afford a trip to the United kingdoms capitol city. Click on the link below and enter your details for this ecslusive deal.

What errors did you spot? Identify these as Spelling, Punctuation or Grammar errors below.

Spelling	Punctuation	Grammar
e.g. easyer	e.g. no full stop	e.g. expression errors

Activity 10 Register

You have been asked to 'improve' the register for the following quotes from visitors to London for a more 'official' leaflet. What changes would you make to the following:

Informal expression	Appropriate register (expression)
The café was OK I s'pose but not the greatest.	The café facilities were adequate but could have been significantly better.
I didn't know what the guide was even on about.	
London is so cool.	
It was AWESOME!!!!!	
The food in London isn't all that.	

Activity 11

Different visitors to a new London attraction called 'Ghost Towers' have written about their experiences. You run a travel website that sells tickets for this attraction and need to choose five short phrases (between four and ten words) for your main web page. Which ones would you choose?

Text A

We were greeted by the Ghost Towers' manager who led us to the new exhibition. With notebooks at the ready, each of us boarded the 'Deadly Drop' ride and attempted to write a review for our corresponding newspapers while clinging on to the barriers! I can assure readers that the rides are totally safe, despite the screams from twenty journalists!

Text B

<u>Saturday 5 May</u> Had an amazing day today! All of class 4 visited Ghost Towers and it was one of the most amazing places that I have ever been to! The coach dropped us off at the Embankment and we had nearly two hours being scared out of our wits on the Towers' rides and their underground maze.

Text C

I would certainly advise an early arrival as we had to queue for nearly two hours. It was worth it though, as the rides were thrilling, the 'ghost walk' was really convincing and the staff were friendly. I would rate Ghost Towers 4 out of 5 stars. ✳✳✳✳

Text D

Dear Manager,

I would like to thank the staff at Ghost Towers for their support and help after my young son became agitated on one of the rides. The operator stopped the ride immediately and was patient and reassuring with us, explaining to my son that the ghosts weren't real and that he could skip the queue and ride again later if he felt like it.

Stretch
List the texts in rank order of likelihood they might appear on your site. Give reasons for your choices.

Test yourself

In the *Daily Mail* article about London, Boris Johnson (the Mayor of London) said:

'These incredible figures prove that London is, without doubt, the greatest city on the planet.'

Write an essay which argues for or against this viewpoint. [20]

Use this planning flowchart to add your own points for or against London being 'the greatest city on the planet'. Once completed, you should be ready to write your essay in full. Remember that you should aim to write 350–500 words.

Top tips

It is very important to decide which viewpoint you want to take. Before starting it may be worth designing a table with arguments **for** and **against** the statement. The longer list will probably be the best viewpoint to take.

Starters

Start with a clear statement of purpose.
- It was of particular interest to me to read that …
- Having visited London on several occasions …
- You do not need to be a frequent visitor to London to know that …

↓

Linking between paragraphs

- Another consideration must be …
- In addition …
- Likewise …
- As a result …
- Furthermore …
- Equally important …

↓

Establishing a point of view

- Firstly, …
- I wholeheartedly agree that …
- The main reason that …
- I simply cannot agree that …
- Surely …
- Without doubt, …
- I recently read that …
- Statistics show that …

↓

Arguing against other opinions – counter-argument

- Contrary to this view, …
- Nevertheless, …
- However, …
- While …
- On the other hand, …
- Conversely, …
- In spite of …
- I doubt …
- Despite the objection that …

↓

Ending your essay with a conclusive statement

- In short, …
- In conclusion, …
- For the reasons outlined, …
- To be sure, …

Useful phrases for argumentation writing

You could consider these useful phrases:

In my personal experience ...

Visitors should consider the fact that ...

Another point is ...

Not only ... but also ...

To strengthen an argument and give a further example:

Furthermore, similarly, moreover ...

To provide a counter-argument:

However, ... on the other hand, ... by contrast, ... conversely, ... despite this, ...

Consider starting some sentences with adverbs:

Strangely, ... Bizarrely, ... Surprisingly, ...

Top tips

1 You can use 'firstly' and 'secondly', but do not go further than this. 'Thirdly', 'fourthly' and 'fifthly' sounds inappropriate.

2 Avoid starting with 'I am writing this essay because ...' as it doesn't sound very engaging.

3 Use the source material or personal experience as a starting point:

The London's Mayor's comments in last Saturday's The Daily Mail were ..., It was of particular interest to me to read that ..., Having visited London on several occasions ..., You do not need to be a frequent visitor to London to know that ...

Stretch

Write a revision page for inclusion in a school study guide for GCSE. This will be an **A4 advice page on how to write a personal essay**. Include information about:

- planning your ideas
- appropriate register and tone
- how to structure your essay
- how to write an introduction and conclusion
- useful sentence starters
- useful phrases to link paragraphs
- punctuation tips
- any other advice which you consider useful.

2c The festival season

Oracy

Learning objectives

In this unit you will be:
- interacting with others;
- responding to questions and ideas;
- practising spoken accuracy;
- drawing ideas together.

Activity 1

A promotions company wants to hold a one-day music festival in your area of the town. It will include local bands and tribute bands from all over the UK, along with stalls selling merchandise and food. These are the details:

- Location: Goodstone Park.
- Festival name: Goodstock.
- Visitors: 3,000.
- Time: final Saturday of August. Midday until midnight.
- Ticket price: £20.
- Number of bands: eight.
- Facilities: marquee, staging, six food vans, five merchandise stalls.
- Amenities: four toilet blocks.
- Security: perimeter fencing around marquee; marshals to check tickets.
- Cost: £70,000. £50,000 to be paid by promoters and made back in ticket sales, with a profit. Remaining £20,000 to be paid by council out of residents' taxes.
- Age restrictions: over-14s only.

1 Consider two advantages and disadvantages of this festival.
2 As a pair can you come up with five points, **either** for or against the festival.
3 In a group of four, spend five minutes putting your case for or against the music festival.

Activity 2

A formal meeting is to be held at Goodstone to discuss whether the festival is going to go ahead.

Look at the roles below:

Your role is a **council representative**.	Your role is a **parent**.
As a member of the town council, you are concerned about the social costs of the festival, such as litter, vandalism and late night noise. The council also has a limited budget.	With two teenagers, you know that they will want to attend the festival but are very reluctant to let them. You fear exposure to alcohol and are worried about what sort of people the festival might attract.
Your role is a **young resident**.	Your role is a **local business person**.
You do not think that there are many facilities for young people in your town and are excited that there will finally be an event held that young people will enjoy.	You own a convenience store next to the proposed festival site. The festival will potentially bring in a lot of money for your store and for the surrounding businesses, which will be good for the town.

Top tips

1 Contribute **regularly** and express your opinion **clearly**.
2 Ask **relevant** questions to other group members.
3 **Listen** and respond fully to their answers – avoid brief answers.
4 Pick up on what others have said and **expand** on their points.
5 Introduce **new** points of your own.
6 If you disagree, **politely** explain why.

1 Choose one role. Spend five minutes jotting down more ideas for or against the festival.

2 Hold your meeting to discuss whether the festival should go ahead. Remember to stay in the role you have been assigned, and put forward the opinions that your character is likely to hold.

3 Come to a final decision as to whether the festival should go ahead. An assigned chairperson should report the final decision and explain the reasons for coming to this decision.

Stretch

Take the role of chairperson and listen sensitively to others' ideas. Your role is to move the discussion forward if it falls flat – or change direction if becoming repetitive or too heated. Try to sum up others' ideas effectively at key points. This is essential for when you report back to the class.

Activity 3 Improving spoken accuracy

Complete the table with improved expressions that are suitable for a formal meeting.

Informal expression	Appropriate register (expression)
I don't get what you're on about.	
He don't live by the park.	
It's grim up by there, innit?	
Them people don't understand.	
It'd be right noisy.	

Activity 4 Individual presentation

You have been asked to give a presentation on your views on introducing a new festival in your school, with proceeds going to charity. Your presentation can argue **for** or **against** the idea, and should last between three and five minutes. (Please note that, for Unit 1 assessment purposes, the individual presentation is expected to last between 5 and 7 minutes - including responses to questions from the audience.)

Think about:

1 The type of festival and why the school should hold the event.

2 When and where it will be held, with details of the suitability of the venue.

3 The volume of festival-goers.

4 How it will be organised and advertised.

5 How the event could benefit both the charity and the school.

6 Any other details of the event.

Sample student responses

Read the opening lines of each student's presentation below. Each one has a different approach but all contain elements of 'good practice'. What elements make these successful?

Sample opening A

I am here today to tell you about why I think our school should hold a Battle of the Bands. Quite simply, this is an event that will take little in terms of organisation and money but will raise a lot for charity. If we hold this event at the end of term, it will give students something to look forward to after their exams and will also promote the school locally because it will show the community that we are a caring school.

Sample opening B

Do you want to enjoy student talent while helping to raise money for charity? If a fun afternoon of quality music and time off from the pressures of school life sounds appealing, then please support our proposal for a Battle of the Bands. We have so many incredibly talented students in our school who would be immensely grateful for the opportunity to showcase their talents while helping worthwhile causes.

Sample opening C

School life is marked by study and exams. Indeed, the role of a school is to educate but I think we also have a social imperative to involve ourselves in the wider community. Student life should not just be marked by improving our subject knowledge, but also by growing as moral and responsible citizens. Holding a charity event in school is a positive way to encourage students to develop a social conscience and is also great fun! We propose holding a Battle of the Bands in order to raise much needed funds for Primrose Hospice, which is only a mile from the school.

Reading

Learning objectives

In this unit you will be:
- retrieving and analysing information;
- comparing ideas in texts;
- identifying facts and opinion;
- evaluating the reliability of a text.

Activity 5

Read the article and answer the questions that follow.

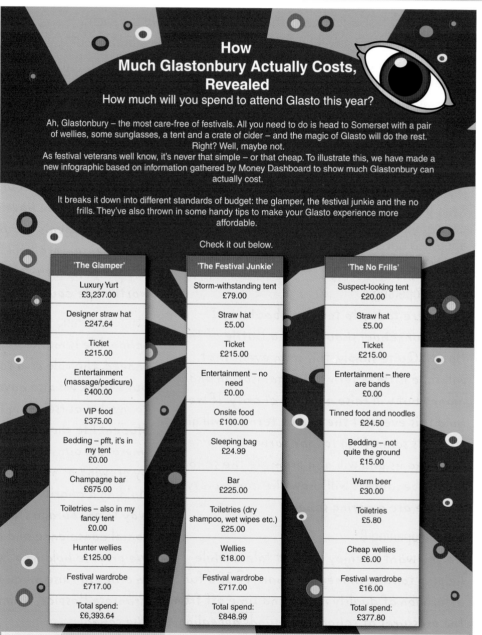

How Much Glastonbury Actually Costs, Revealed

How much will you spend to attend Glasto this year?

Ah, Glastonbury – the most care-free of festivals. All you need to do is head to Somerset with a pair of wellies, some sunglasses, a tent and a crate of cider – and the magic of Glasto will do the rest. Right? Well, maybe not.

As festival veterans well know, it's never that simple – or that cheap. To illustrate this, we have made a new infographic based on information gathered by Money Dashboard to show much Glastonbury can actually cost.

It breaks it down into different standards of budget: the glamper, the festival junkie and the no frills. They've also thrown in some handy tips to make your Glasto experience more affordable.

Check it out below.

'The Glamper'	'The Festival Junkie'	'The No Frills'
Luxury Yurt £3,237.00	Storm-withstanding tent £79.00	Suspect-looking tent £20.00
Designer straw hat £247.64	Straw hat £5.00	Straw hat £5.00
Ticket £215.00	Ticket £215.00	Ticket £215.00
Entertainment (massage/pedicure) £400.00	Entertainment – no need £0.00	Entertainment – there are bands £0.00
VIP food £375.00	Onsite food £100.00	Tinned food and noodles £24.50
Bedding – pfft, it's in my tent £0.00	Sleeping bag £24.99	Bedding – not quite the ground £15.00
Champagne bar £675.00	Bar £225.00	Warm beer £30.00
Toiletries – also in my fancy tent £0.00	Toiletries (dry shampoo, wet wipes etc.) £25.00	Toiletries £5.80
Hunter wellies £125.00	Wellies £18.00	Cheap wellies £6.00
Festival wardrobe £717.00	Festival wardrobe £717.00	Festival wardrobe £16.00
Total spend: £6,393.64	Total spend: £848.99	Total spend: £377.80

Affordable Festival tips:
1. Book your train tickets as far in advance as possible. Prices on the day can easily go well above £100 for a return ticket. Or, if you have time to spare, opt for a coach instead as it'll work out much cheaper.
2. Be strategic about your clothing. Instead of buying five sets of clothing plus items you might need in case the weather starts playing up, invest in one comfortable and light set of clothing that can last you for five days.
3. Take cash. We'd advise you withdrawing money before you get to the festival – the cash-machines on site will charge you for the transaction. It's also easier to cap your spending on food and drinks when you know exactly how much money you have to spend.

1 Select two words in the opening paragraph that suggest the festival experience is positive.

2 The writer categorises three types of festival goer, 'the glamper, the festival junkie and the no frills'. What do you think the writer means by each type?

3 Identify two examples of sarcasm in 'the Glamper' column.

4 The information in tip 2 refers to being 'strategic'. Select **one** definition from the list below that best defines this.
   a thoughtful
   b planning to advantage
   c considerate
   d organised and methodical

5 Explain what is meant by 'cap your spending'.

Activity 6 Editorial skills

Read the paragraph below and then answer the questions that follow:

Glastonbury has a .....(1)..... for being the most diverse festival in the UK. What makes the event truly .....(2)..... is its rich history.

1 Choose the word below that best fits gap (1):
   a notion
   b reputation
   c position
   d role

2 Choose the word below that best fits gap (2):
   a legendary
   b predictable
   c eccentric
   d classical

Activity 7

The following sentences are in the wrong order. **Sequence** the sentences into a logical order:

1 On arrival at the festival site, visitors had their faces scanned before entry.

2 Despite this opposition, the technology is likely to be used by other festivals across the UK.

3 These facial images were then compared with a database of custody images across Europe.

4 Security has been stepped-up at Leicester's Download rock festival this year.

5 Festival-goers generally opposed the scans, calling them an invasion of privacy.

Activity 8

The exam may test your ability to separate fact from opinion. Test your understanding by working through these examples. Then look at Activity 9.

Statement	Fact or opinion?
Canberra is the capital city of Australia.	
Cristiano Ronaldo is the best football player of all time.	
Winston Churchill was a British prime minister.	
Disneyworld, Florida is the greatest holiday destination in the world.	
Social media has improved people's lives.	

Activity 9

1 Read the following extract about the Download rock music festival.

Download is the UK's premier rock festival. It is held at Donnington Park in Leicestershire. The first Download festival was held in 2003 and attended by over 50,000 fans who loved every minute. With weekend tickets starting at £170, the price is fantastic value for money.

2 Identify two facts and two opinions in the text.

Activity 10

Read through Texts A and B opposite, then look at these questions. Discuss which question is the easier to answer (based on the text). Explain why one question is more difficult to answer than the other.

1 According to the article, what attitudes do people have towards music festivals? (Text A)

2 Explain why the writer hates festivals. (Text B)

Text A: Music festivals: the sound of escapism

Why do people love festivals – is it the music? Or a place to forget your rubbish job? Dr Andrew Bengry-Howell of the University of Bath, managed to persuade 98 people at four of the UK's largest music festivals to have a chat about what they got out of attending a live music event. Having expected them to rave about the music, the message he got was that festivals were a way to help them to cope with their increasingly dull and stressful lives.

'One person said that, without music festivals, there'd be no point in living in this country at all,' he recalls.

'Others talked about freedom and being able to totally forget about your rubbish job in a call centre. Many started talking about the pressure they felt under and about seeing festivals as a haven.'

There was a sense of release in being able to drift aimlessly and not feel guilty while inside the protected 'world' of the festival site. Some said they tried to 'disappear' into a festival and would purposely leave their mobile phones at home.

The overall message was that festivals provided an escape for young people who felt ground down by the constant pressure to achieve, and the sense they got from society that it was their personal failure if they didn't manage to make the grade – financially, socially and on the career ladder.

'I'm interested in this idea about festivals being where people go to experience a kind of freedom, and that they feel so restricted, even though we now have more freedoms than ever,' said Bengry-Howell.

www.theguardian.com/education/2011

Text B: Music festivals: Why do we do it? By Tony Naylor

Are you rigid with excitement at Glastonbury? Ticking the days off until V? No, me neither. Mainly because live music is best kept indoors.

Call me miserable – you wouldn't be the first – but I *hate* music festivals.

I hate camping. I hate not showering. I hate drinking watery lager-like fluid out of waxy cups. I hate listening to bands outside on wind-blown sound systems. I hate portaloos. I hate mud. I hate being trapped in the middle of nowhere. I hate every band (e.g. Foo Fighters, Kaiser Chiefs) that has ever been dubbed a 'great festival band'.

I hate the dreary, risk-free predictability of most British festival lineups. I hate middle-class students shouting from tent-to-tent at 4am. I hate their middle-class parents parking Winnebagos* in the VIP bit. I hate paying crazy prices for life's essentials. I hate the food. I hate corporate sponsorship. I hate thirty-something professionals for whom Bestival is their one big annual trip. I hate the whole myth of the transforming 'festival experience'. I even hate watching Colin Murray and Jo Whiley drone on about how [insert your least favourite HMV indie band here] played 'the most amazing set' of the weekend.

Our grandparents fought wars, formed unions, scrimped and saved in order that we might have indoor toilets, running water and nightclubs with cloakrooms and crystal clear *Funktion One* sound systems. And what do we do? We go to Glastonbury and live like 18th century peasants.

www.theguardian.com/music

* A Winnebago is a large camper van.

Stretch

Use the following success criteria to peer-mark responses to this question:

- Does the answer link across both texts?
- Is there a range of evidence used from both texts?
- Does the answer have a clear focus on the question?
- Does the answer address the writers' techniques?

If these criteria are met, then this indicates a high band response.

Test yourself

Compare how the writers present festivals in Text A and Text B. You must refer to both texts to support your comments on the language the writers have used. [10]

Top tips

When texts are so dissimilar, it is a good idea to start with a clear **overview** that sums up the writer's intentions in each text. This will signal to the examiner that you have understood each text as a whole in relation to each other.

Useful words for comparing texts:

While ...   However ...   In contrast to ...   Conversely ...
On the other hand ...   More ...   Less ...

Read the students' responses to this activity below. Decide which is the more effective and why. Think about the following:

- Where do the students give a sense of **overview**?
- How is evidence from the text used?
- How does the writer link across both texts?

Sample student responses

Student A

Text A explains why people love festivals so much and gives reasons for people's need to visit these events, whereas Text B is a sarcastic attack on festivals.

The first text begins with rhetorical questions which shows that the article is going to explore people's motivations for going to the festival. In order to come to a decision, the writer has asked a range of people for their ideas and uses direct speech to support his ideas. Conversely, the second article only looks at giving his opinion of festivals and doesn't use any third person opinions ...

Examiner comment:

So far, the response begins with a good overview and confidently links ideas across both texts. The answer also looks at issues of 'technique'. However, there is a lack of focus in the answer as the candidate appears to be looking generally at how the writers express their ideas rather than focusing on how **festivals** are presented.

Student B

The writers present festivals in different ways. Text A contains evidence to show that people enjoy festivals as it they are an escape from the boredom of their working lives. Text B takes a very different view to this. The writer presents this kind of living as being 'like 18th century peasants', rather than an escape.

In Text A, the writer includes a quotation which gives an exaggerated opinion of festivals; one person says that without festivals there would 'be no point in living in this country at all'. Text B, in contrast, gives lots of opinions such as 'I hate festivals'. This takes a totally different viewpoint.

Examiner comment:

This starts very confidently and gives a clear overview here. There is also skilful linking across the texts AND a clear focus on the question. However, this is too brief to reach into the higher bands.

Writing

Activity 11 Put it to the proof

Fake reviews posted on websites compromise the credibility of the site. If a description of an event is not genuine, readers will not trust the website. Read the following review. Find all the errors in the text that show you that this is not a genuine review.

> *I found an eciting time in Manchester. We went to Musuem of Sience and Industry which was inovative and filled with many artifacts. The range of exibits in the museum was Incredible. Theres a massive fossil of a dinosaur and creepy mummys from egyptian time's I also recommend that you go see the japenese spider crab.*

What sort of errors did you spot? Identify these as Spelling, Punctuation or Grammar errors below.

Spelling	Punctuation	Grammar
e.g. Musuem	e.g. no full stop	e.g. expression errors

Activity 12

Read the website entry overleaf from a resident who has decided to **describe** their experiences at a festival held in their town and submit it to a local 'What's on?' website.

Try to find the following techniques in the text and consider how they are used:

Use of pronouns	Look at how first (I) and second person (you) are used.
Evaluative adjectives	Describing words which suggest a 'value', e.g. great.
Exclamatives	Sentences which end in '!'
Adverb starters	e.g. *firstly, unfortunately* placed at start of sentences.
Proper nouns	Nouns for names of things – start with capitals.
Facts and statistics	Specific details to inform readers.

There was music in the air at Romilly Park last weekend, as the GlastonBarry festival took place. Hearing that the organisers, Ross Mackintosh and Matthew Blumberg, had spent nine months planning the sell-out event, I thought that I should be one of the 2000 music fans from across the UK that descended on our town to hear their favourite tribute bands and experience some top quality festival fun.

The event sold out in nine days! Apparently, more than 500 people were left on a waiting list hoping for tickets. I got in early and bought my tickets two months ago! I think that £25 for two days is pretty affordable, especially when you consider that the really big festivals charge hundreds of pounds. Chatting to festival-goers on the day, I came across music fans who were willing to travel from as far away as Leicester to enjoy a weekend of music at a bargain price.

OK – the bands were tribute acts and not the real thing, but this was, of course, reflected in the much cheaper price than you'd pay somewhere like Glastonbury, Reading or Leeds. Personally, I thought the bands were incredible! Europe's number one Bob Marley tribute band – *Legend* – played for over an hour. Led Zeppelin act, *The Hindenburgs*, played classic tunes and got the whole marquee rocking. Everyone had a great time!

The event was so well-organised and professional, yet – and I'm going to say it again – it was a fraction of the price of other UK festivals! Big name tribute groups like *Oashish* played here, but there's room for the local bands too. I'll be back next year, and, if you're a music lover, you should go too.

Activity 13

What words and phrases make this sound like an informal review? How would you alter the last two paragraphs for a more **formal** website?

Stretch

Intensifying your writing

You can convey your point of view more strongly by using well-chosen intensifiers (types of adverb) to exaggerate the adjective. For example: <u>outrageously</u> late, <u>ridiculously</u> loud.

Choose an intensifier to go with each of the words in the table below. They can be positive or negative.

Intensifier	Adjective
monstrously	noisy
	irritating
	inconsiderate
	intelligent
	stereotypical
	intriguing

Test yourself

Imagine that the music festival you discussed earlier in the section has taken place. After attending the event you decide to write a review to **describe** the event for an entertainment website. [35]

Planning

For a 'describe' task it is useful to write about your experiences in **sections**. Each paragraph may focus on a particular aspect, for example the venue, the food, the bands, the merchandise.

You can end with a summary or recommendation.

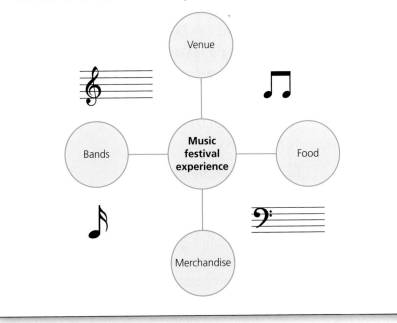

Top tips

1 This is a personal review, so you can use first person 'I' or 'we'.

2 Consider your form, purpose and audience. This is an independent review so there is no need to write persuasively. Your readers could be of any age, but teenagers and young people are more likely to attend festivals. A more relaxed register would therefore be appropriate.

3 If it is easier you can organise your website with subheadings, using, for example, alliteration (*Festival Fun!*), rhyme (*Can't Stand the Band?*) or a pun/play on words (*If music be the food of love – STOP RIGHT NOW!*). Your plan should help you to turn each section into a **header** or **topic sentence starter**.

Sample student responses

Decide which is the more effective and why.

Student A

There were certainly smiles on the faces of the crowd at Larks in the Park last Saturday, but for myself and all the other under-twenties of the town, there were only frowns.

Grangetown's Youth Group have campaigned for months for a festival and been told by Goodstone Council that it would cost too much and would bring disruption to the area. Surprisingly, these concerns were swept aside when Larks in the Park over-fifties music day was approved.

Tempted by cheap train tickets, hundreds of the visitors were able to use their bus and train passes to travel to the event. Apparently there were picnics, craft stalls and even a tea-tent, all for the bargain price of £15 for the day.

My nan loved it and has talked about the day ever since. She's told me that Frankly Sinatra brought a smile to her face, with more excitement when Surely Bassey and The Three 'Tenners' hit the stage. The event was certainly popular, with hundreds of older people in attendance, but the fact that it was held at all seems grossly unfair when schools, youth clubs and sports' clubs have all campaigned for a youth music festival.

Last term, our own school student group wrote to Goodstone's councillors, asking for a youth festival to be held in the town. The council replied with a dismissive email saying that, 'Money raised by local taxes needs to go to services that will benefit the whole town and not just young people.' However, this claim was clearly ignored where Larks in the Park was concerned. I'm not against our town having a senior sing-a-long; it would just be nice if there's something for young people next year.

So far, it's GOLDEN OLDIES — 1 TEENAGERS — 0.

Examiner comment:

This is engaging and creative, with the idea of a festival for older people being an original approach to the task. There is a range of effective techniques, with the alliteration of 'senior sing-a-long' and clever use of the final 'score card' result. Use of opposites in 'smiles' and 'frowns' shows confidence. An appropriate use of register is adapted to suit the task's audience and purpose. There is a range of sentence structures, with a high degree of accuracy. The review is typical of work in the higher bands.

Student B

I am so pleased that a music festival has finally been held in the town. I attended myself last weekend and have to say that it was a graet event with thousands of people there. The tickets were only £20 which is a little bit expensive but not too bad. You got 8 bands for that price – you also got food stalls and ice-cream vans. These were selling hot-dogs, burgers, drinks, chocolate, sweets and other snacks.

There was allsorts of music, like pop, rock, hip hop, rap, dance and techno. This is a good vareity for only £20. The bands played for an hour each and the sound was good quality.

Some people did not want the festival to be held. A local man called Bob Harrison did not want it. I interviewed him and he said 'I live across the road from this park and I can hear the music allover my house and it's really annoying,' However I also interviewed a young person called Amy White who said 'I think it's amazing that this festival is being held in the town because there's nothing to do here and it's about time we had something.'

The festival cost allot of money to organise but it was worth it becuase so many people went and they all loved it. It was only £20 which is a good price.

Overall this was a wonderfully satisfying experience!

Examiner comment:

The writing is generally coherent and appropriate to the task. The review of the event is fairly convincing and there are some apt details. Phrases such as, 'I interviewed him' and 'this is a good variety' are a little clumsy. The ticket price is mentioned three times which suggests that the student is struggling for ideas at times. There is some attempt to use a range of vocabulary ('attended', 'satisfying') but there are some spelling and grammatical errors. This work is more typical of a mid-band response.

Unit 3: The world of science and technology

3a Technology in schools

Oracy

Learning objectives

In this unit you will be:
- interacting with others;
- drawing ideas together;
- responding to others' ideas;
- using a formal situation.

Activity 1

You have been asked to feedback to the school governors on the benefits and disadvantages of technology in your school.

In your groups, think about all the areas where technology is used in your school and who uses this technology.

Activity 2

As a group, consider what are the advantages and disadvantages of using technology in schools.

Your group may want to consider some, or all, of the following statements collected from a questionnaire given out to students:

'I love it when we use the iPads as it really helps me learn.'

'I couldn't live without my mobile phone.'

'I can't use my mobile phone to do research – it is so frustrating!'

'Whiteboards help to engage learners.'

'Too much time is wasted in computer rooms.'

'We should be able to use spell checkers in exams.'

'We are able to do homework online and get in touch with teachers from home.'

'We could use technology much more.'

Statements from a questionnaire given out to staff:

'Mobile phones are a big distraction in class.'

'I don't feel confident in using my whiteboard; it is just a glorified projector screen.'

'Standards of writing have fallen over the past ten years, so technology has not had a positive impact.'

'Learners are relying too much on electronic spell checkers and these are impeding ability to check.'

'I could not teach without technology.'

'Technology has made pupils safer.'

'Online classrooms make it much easier to check pupil progress.'

'My best lessons have involved technology but it is not always easy to coordinate.'

'I feel that we, in schools, are way behind the outside world and the students themselves.'

Statements from a questionnaire given out to parents:

'My son seems to spend most of his time on computer games – I can't get him to do his homework at all!'

'It is much easier to contact teachers now via email.'

'I love the reminders I get via text messages from the school.'

'My daughter says that they hardly ever put pen to paper any more – that can't help her when it comes to exams.'

'It's ridiculous that they are buying tablets but they haven't got enough money to have a textbook each.'

'I like the cashless system in my child's school – I can see exactly what he's spending and when.'

'I feel safer knowing that my daughter has a mobile phone to ring me on in an emergency.'

'My son had terrible trouble from bullying on a social media site.'

Activity 3

Discuss whether technology in schools is a good or bad thing. Adopt one of the following roles, ensuring that each of these is covered by at least one person:

- a teacher
- a pupil
- a parent.

Discuss the pros and cons of technology in schools from the viewpoint of your role.

Stretch

As a group, present a verbal report to the Governing Body, outlining the pros and cons of technology in your school and where investment should be made in the future.

Your report should use standard English, be balanced and provide supporting evidence and reasons for your conclusion.

Reading

Text A: extract from a secondary school's Acceptable Use Agreement for pupils using ICT

Dear Parent/Carer,

ICT including the internet, learning platforms/websites, email and mobile technologies has become an important part of learning in our school. We expect all pupils to be safe and responsible when using any ICT. It is essential that pupils are aware of eSafety and know how to stay safe when using any ICT.

Pupils are expected to read and discuss this agreement with their parent or carer and then to sign and follow the terms of the agreement. Any concerns or explanation can be discussed with their class teacher or Mr Lashley, the school's eSafety coordinator.

Please return this form to school for filing.

Text B: Extract from a newspaper article in 'The Telegraph' on a report into the use of technology in schools, by Madhumita Murgia

Technology in classrooms doesn't make students smarter

A global study by OECD finds that more digital devices in schools does not equal better performance

Computers do not noticeably improve school children's academic results and can even hamper performance, according to a report that looked at the impact of technology in classrooms across the globe.

While nearly three-quarters of all the students surveyed from 64 different countries said they used a computer at school, the report by the Organisation for Economic Cooperation and Development (OECD) found that technology had made no improvement in results.

In fact, in countries that reported the most technology use in the classroom, such as Spain, Sweden and Australia, students' reading performance actually declined between 2000 and 2012.

In South Korea and Hong Kong, students used computers for an average of roughly 10 minutes at school – just a fraction of the full hour spent on the internet by Australian students, for instance.

Conversely, in these Asian countries where less than half the students reported using computers at school, the children were among the top performers in reading and computer-based mathematics tests, according to OECD's assessment program.

The report did not recommend using less technology in classrooms, but instead rethinking how it was implemented. While digital textbooks and online mathematics problems work well, copying and pasting text from the web wasn't as useful.

'In the end, technology can amplify great teaching, but great technology cannot replace poor teaching,' Schleicher said.

www.telegraph.co.uk/technology

Text B (continued)

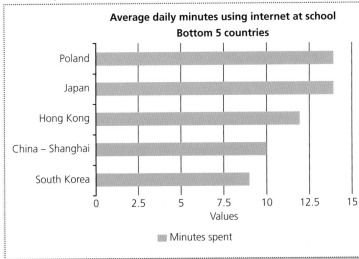

Average daily minutes using internet at school
Bottom 5 countries

Text D

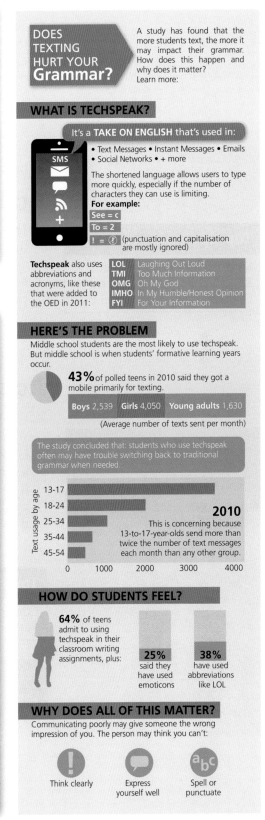

DOES TEXTING HURT YOUR Grammar?

A study has found that the more students text, the more it may impact their grammar. How does this happen and why does it matter? Learn more:

WHAT IS TECHSPEAK?

It's a **TAKE ON ENGLISH** that's used in:

- Text Messages • Instant Messages • Emails
- Social Networks • + more

The shortened language allows users to type more quickly, especially if the number of characters they can use is limiting.
For example:
See = c
To = 2
! = ! (punctuation and capitalisation are mostly ignored)

Techspeak also uses abbreviations and acronyms, like these that were added to the OED in 2011:

LOL	Laughing Out Loud
TMI	Too Much Information
OMG	Oh My God
IMHO	In My Humble/Honest Opinion
FYI	For Your Information

HERE'S THE PROBLEM

Middle school students are the most likely to use techspeak. But middle school is when students' formative learning years occur.

43% of polled teens in 2010 said they got a mobile primarily for texting.

| Boys 2,539 | Girls 4,050 | Young adults 1,630 |

(Average number of texts sent per month)

The study concluded that: students who use techspeak often may have trouble switching back to traditional grammar when needed.

2010
This is concerning because 13-to-17-year-olds send more than twice the number of text messages each month than any other group.

HOW DO STUDENTS FEEL?

64% of teens admit to using techspeak in their classroom writing assignments, plus:

25% said they have used emoticons

38% have used abbreviations like LOL

WHY DOES ALL OF THIS MATTER?

Communicating poorly may give someone the wrong impression of you. The person may think you can't:

Think clearly — Express yourself well — Spell or punctuate

Text C: Contribution from a teacher on an education forum (TES)

Mobile phone jammers

Discussion in 'Behaviour' started by
joedoggyuk, 21/5/2015

I had a lazy 14-year-old ask me what time I'd be leaving school (bit suspicious, but he hasn't the brains or discipline to hatch any devious plan against me); when I told him 7pm (ended up being 8) he laughed and took pleasure in knowing his day was done at 3.

Anyway, I need to retaliate.

The real weakness of these kids is their addiction: their phones.

I could try and ban them (phones, not teenagers) in class, but there's no use sailing against a prevailing wind.

A mobile phone jammer would cut them off, make them go cold turkey. Best of all they'd have no idea it was me cutting them off from their social lives. They might get some more work done too.

It's illegal to operate a phone jammer in the UK. Despite this, there must be other teachers out there who have either beaten me to it, or who have thought about it.

It's got to be easier than the daily battle against phones. Besides, I get a kick out of outsmarting children so badly they don't even realise they've been outsmarted.

https://community.tes.com

Activity 4

1 Text A is an example of which kind of text? (See page 172 in the 'Busting the jargon' section at the end of this book for an explanation of these terms.)
   a personal
   b public
   c occupational
   d educational?

2 Look at Text A. **Identify** two reasons why the school considers it necessary to have an 'Acceptable Use Agreement for ICT'.

Activity 5

1 Text B uses the word 'Conversely'. **Select** one definition from the list below that best defines this word:
   a On the other hand
   b Also
   c Again
   d Another point is

2 Look at Text B. **Explain** how the article supports the view that 'Technology doesn't make us smarter'.

Activity 6

1 Look at Text C. What is the viewpoint of the writer? How is this viewpoint created?

2 Look at Text D. Which of these statements is the odd one out?
   a Girls send more texts than boys.
   b 'Humble' and 'honest' can both stand for the 'h' in IMHO.
   c 18–24-year-olds send more texts than any other age group.
   d 38 per cent of teens have admitted to using text abbreviations like LOL in their school assignments.

Top tips

Find the word in the text. Read the sentence around the word.

Stretch

Write a reply to the forum thread on Text C which gives an opposing view with support.

Top tips

Consider each statement. Cross reference each one against the text and see what connects three of them.

Stretch

Use Text D to make up more odd-one-out questions.

Activity 7

Rank the four texts in terms of their reliability. Explain why you have ordered them in this way.

Top tips

Think about what makes a text reliable:

1 Who has written it?
2 Where does it appear?
3 What format does it use?
4 How many people have looked at it before publication?
5 What amount and range of factual evidence is used?
6 Is the writer biased?

Try asking these questions of the texts presented here. You may not be able to answer all of them, but they will help you organise your thoughts to begin answering Question 4 and access more of the marks in higher tariff questions.

What affected your decisions? What made one text more reliable than the other?

Stretch

Reread Texts A to D. What are the disadvantages and advantages of using technology presented across all the texts?

Sample student responses

Student A

I think the first text is the most reliable because it is a school agreement about the use of ICT and it is written in a very formal way. This is shown by the opening 'Dear parent/Carer'. The fact that it is to be 'filed' for future use makes it sound like a legal document. There is no real bias in the letter as it is only asking for a contract signature from parents. There are also formal titles used for people and that makes it sound more official and trustworthy.

Examiner comment:

This is a higher band response as it refers to the form and audience (parent/carer) of the letter. The student has shown a focus on the question by referring to the issue of what makes it reliable (very formal, legal document, no bias, official, trustworthy) throughout. The student has also included a range of examples from the text. The clear focus and examples selected make this a confident response.

Student B

I think the first text is most reliable because it is addressed to parents and they have to sign it to show they have read it. It is also a short agreement which is politely written and the fact that it is written in school makes it sound more reliable.

Examiner comment:

This is a lower band response as it refers to the audience (parents) of the letter and indicates the purpose. However, there is not enough use of support evidence from the text and not enough focus on what makes it reliable. It is 'politely' written but there are no examples used and the final comment is too general and not strictly accurate.

Writing

Learning objectives

In this unit you will be:
- adapting your style, register and vocabulary to write a report;
- developing proofreading skills;
- communicating ideas clearly and effectively in report writing;
- developing argumentation writing skills.

Activity 8 Thinking about reports

- Where do we come across reports in life? What examples can you think of?
- What are the aims of a report? Who is the target audience? Is it a public, personal, educational or occupational text?

Activity 9

Look at the text below, which is an extract from a report:

Report on Technology Use in School

From: ICT Committee

To: Headteacher

Date: March 2016

This report aims to outline the current use of technology in school and suggest areas of improvement.

ICT Rooms

These are currently being used at 70% capacity. This means that they are empty for a big proportion of time. Teacher questionnaires reveal that a number of staff feel underqualified in the use of the programs and lack confidence in this area. They also report finding it hard to keep pupils 'on-task'. However, many teachers and pupils who use the ICT suites on a regular basis feel that it helps pupil progress.

Recommendations:

- Introduce a rolling training for training to staff in order to upskill them in the use of various computer programs.

- Introduce a way for teachers to monitor pupils' screens from a central monitor.

---

1   What features does this report have in terms of the format?
2   What features does this report have in terms of the writing style?
3   Write the next item on the report. Try to follow the same tone and style as the beginning.

Activity 10

Below are two excerpts from model reports to give you ideas on the tone, features and layout. Evaluate which is the more effective and why. You can copy and complete the table that is provided after Text B, to compare the success of the two reports.

Text A

Report on Technology Use in School

From: ICT Committee

To: Headteacher

Date: March 2016

This report outlines the main findings and recommendations of the ICT Committee in terms of the use of technology in school and possible areas of development.

1 Mobile phones

Mobile phones are a cause of low-level disruption in over 25% of lessons according to teacher and learner surveys. A minority of teachers say that mobile phones are useful in lessons for learners to access Google and other search engines or to use apps such as calculators and dictionaries. There is a high level of frustration among learners that they cannot use mobile phones for educational purposes in lessons.

Recommendations:

- Use INSET training time in schools to model ways of using mobile phones for learning purposes.
- Update the school policy on the use of mobile phones in lessons.
- Revise sanctions on mobile phone misuse among pupils.

2 Interactive Whiteboards

The school has made a big investment in installing Interactive Whiteboards in every classroom. However, the committee reports that they are not being used effectively in a majority of lessons. Where they are being used effectively, features include spotlighting, literacy (e.g. anagram and question generators) and numeracy features (e.g. graph papers and measuring tools). Visualisers are a useful way of sharing pupils' work and evaluating as a class (with annotation). Feedback suggests that learners react positively to Interactive Whiteboards when they are used properly.

Recommendations:

- Use INSET training time for sharing of good practice between teachers when using the whiteboard.
- Encourage departments to evaluate how well they are using interactive technology.
- Invest in more interactive technology, allowing whole classes to contribute to one document at the same time.

Conclusions:

The ICT Committee hopes that this report is useful in shaping the future direction of technology in the school. Further clarification can be provided on any of these points if required. In addition, the Committee aims to provide a follow-up report in a year's time to evaluate and report on the progress made in our recommendations.

Text B

Report to the Headteacher on technology in schools   **March 2016**

There are 4 main areas where technology is used in schools – these include phones, computers, laptops and tablets and cashless system.

There are lots of areas of improvement that can be made. For example, there are not enough iPads to go around and the school needs to buy more of them.

Also, mobile phones are causing a lot of hassle to people in schools and they need to be banned completely in my opinion.

Another area that is working well is the cashless system for paying for school dinners and trips and things. This means that people on free school dinners are not singled out with tickets.

Finally, the computer rooms are not great. There are broken computers and seats and they take ages to log on the internet and they crash all the time so the school needs to sort this out.

Thank you for reading my report.

Yours sincerely

The ICT Panel.

	Layout	Language features	Tone
Text A	Uses bullets.		
Text B		Uses 'Yours sincerely', which suggests this is a letter rather than a report.	

Activity 11 Put it to the proof

The following school report has been written by a pupil's form teacher. The Head of Year has been tasked with proofreading the reports before they go out to parents/carers. Identify and correct any errors in Spelling, Punctuation or Grammar (there are 10 in total).

I have always known Aaron to be a very well-behaved and courteous young man. He is a very poplar member of the class and is usually punctual and polite

With all this in mind I was very surprised to read some of the comments in this report from Aarons' subject teachers. Quite what possessed Aaron to behave like that with a Bunsen burner is beyond me. I shall also gloss over her treatment of the french student, but I am glad that there is no permenent damage.

I am pleased that Aaron has deal with these issues and I hope he finds a return to form as he moves on to the next year of his studys I wish him luck in this.

What errors did you spot? Identify these as Spelling, Punctuation or Grammar errors below.

Spelling	Punctuation	Grammar
e.g. poplar	e.g. no full stop	e.g. expression errors

Stretch

As Head of Year, what advice would you give this teacher in order to improve his/her literacy?

Test yourself

Read the following exam-style question carefully:

The Headteacher is considering banning all mobile technology in your school, based on evidence of the success of other schools that have taken this step.

Write a report which argues for or against this proposal. [20]

As with all the other extended writing tasks in this book, it is important to PLAN your response.

A useful plan for a report is to think of four or five topic headings.

Think about:

1 the reason for writing the report – set out the aims;

2 the advantages that mobile technology can offer;

3 the disadvantages of mobile technology;

4 findings and/or recommendations.

For example:

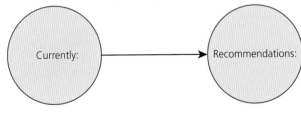

Technology in neighbouring school

Currently: Recommendations:

3b Technology: good or bad?

Oracy

Stretch

As a group, discuss whether technology has made our lives better or worse than our forebearers' lives.

Activity 1

You have been asked to develop an exhibition entitled: 'Inventions That Changed The World' for the British Science Museum. To help you develop your ideas you have been give a series of images.

Discuss what each image shown here represents, and rank order them in terms of the benefits they have given to humans.

Activity 2

Prepare a series of questions you could ask an older family member about the changes in technology that they have seen in their lifetime. Focus on the advantages and disadvantages.

For homework, interview your family member and record their responses using a method of your choice (written, aural or video recording). Bring in your findings to feed into Activity 5's task.

Activity 3

In the box below is a speech that a student gave on whether technology is a good or bad thing. As a group, summarise each point that the student makes and try to recreate the notes he or she prepared before giving the speech.

Sample student response

Today, we live in the 'age of technology'. From high-tech cars to 3-D printers, new inventions are seemingly created every day. You'd think we would be the happiest generation ever, but all too often I hear my grandmother say: 'It's not as good as back in my day.' So is this true?

It is hard for us teenagers to imagine a world without the internet, mobile phones and laptops. But even twenty years ago, these things were not commonplace. Sure, it's great that we can stay in constant touch with our friends and family; search for any bit of information we require; and download music from the comfort of our own sofa. But are we better spellers and more sociable, or has this technology made us more introverted and prone to online bullies and abuse? I certainly am guilty of texting or using social media instead of actually having a conversation with my family.

So this raises the question, are we a society too centered on technology? Let's remember all the good that technology has done. We are able to save hundreds of lives with organ transplants and updated safety measures in vehicles. Advancements in medicines and hospital equipment means that there are thousands of people walking around because of advances in technology. If they had been born a generation previously, they would be dead. But is living longer a good thing? It puts pressure on resources and means over 70 per cent of people will have to work longer and see their children's inheritance dribbling away over many years of care.

Another point to consider is: do we rely upon technology too much? Many of us cannot even drive anywhere without using a GPS to give us directions. How could we survive without central heating, microwaves and washing machines? While our grandparents did, it seems as though we could not.

Of course we have always had new technology. The wheel was once a new technology! Explorers in the past relied on maps and compasses. We cannot stop progress, but we don't necessarily have to think it's all for the better.

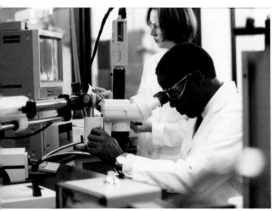

Activity 4

Look at the speech again. What features of good speaking does it use? See if you can identify where the following features are used:

attention-grabbing start *friendly tone* *directly addresses the audience*

personal anecdote *statistics* *humour*

clear points *quote* *questions used*

tripling *connecting words and phrases used*

Activity 5

As a group, aim to present the three best things and the three worst things about the advances in technology over the last 100 years. When you have reached some conclusions as a group, present your findings to the class, being careful to support your ideas with clear reasons.

There are various approaches you can take, but you may like to list the advantages and disadvantages related to the following technologies:

- motor vehicles and travel;
- technology linked to health and treatments of diseases;
- communication;
- nuclear energy;
- computers.

Try to use as many good features of oracy from Activity 4 as possible!

Reading

Learning objectives

In this unit you will be:

- distinguishing between facts and opinions, and statements that are supported and those which are not;
- evaluating the reliability of texts;
- making inferences and deductions.

Text A: Extract from Linus Pauling's diary. It discusses his conversation with Albert Einstein on 16 November 1954

On 16 November 1954 I talked with Albert Einstein at his home in Princeton, for a couple of hours, about various matters, scientific in part, but especially about the world as a whole.

When I said goodbye, and left the house, I stopped on the sidewalk and wrote two sentences in my notebook, in order that I would not forget just what he had said to me. One statement that he made that I noted is the following … 'You would be astonished to know with how little wisdom the world is governed.'

The other sentence about which I made a note is the following: 'I made one great mistake in my life – when I signed the letter to President Roosevelt recommending that atom bombs be made; but there was some justification – the danger that the Germans would make them.'

http://scarc.library.oregonstate.edu

Text B

ALL OF THE WORLD'S NUKES

COUNTRY	DEPLOYED WARHEADS*	TOTAL 2014	YEAR OF FIRST NUCLEAR TEST
● USA	1,922	7,506	1945
● RUSSIA	2,484	8,484	1949
● UNITED KINGDOM	160	225	1952
● FRANCE	290	300	1960
● CHINA	---	250	1964
● INDIA	80-100	80-100	1974
● PAKISTAN	---	90-110	1998
● ISRAEL	---	80-200	1979
● NORTH KOREA	---	< 10	2006
TOTAL ESTIMATED NUCLEAR WEAPONS: ~17,000			

* Deployed: warheads placed on missiles or located on bases with operational forces.
All estimates are approximate and are as of April 2014.

HIROSHIMA was the first city in history to be the target of a nuclear weapon. The U.S. dropped an atomic bomb at 8:15 a.m. on Aug. 6, 1945, toward the end of World War II.

NAGASAKI was the second and, to date, last city in the world to experience a nuclear attack. That bomb was dropped on Aug. 9, 1945, **instantly killing an estimated 40,000 people.**

70,000+
nuclear warheads and bombs were built between 1945 and 1990.

11 U.S. nuclear bombs have been lost in accidents and never recovered.

The U.S. has reduced its stockpile by 84% from a Cold War peak of 31,255 warheads in 1967.

BUSINESS INSIDER

Sources: U.S. Department of Defense; Center for Defense Information;
Greenpeace; "Lost Bombs," Atwood-Keeney Productions, Inc; U.S. Department of Energy;
Natural Resources Defense Council, Nuclear Weapons Databook Project; Nuclear Threat Initiative

Text C: A visit to the dentist

(extract from *I Remember When I Was Young*, Rob Horlock (Unlimited Publishing, 2014))

Nigel Withers in Dublin still has the occasional flashback to his youthful visits to the dentist.

Pedal power

Our dentist's name was Mr Lamb, I think, but he certainly wasn't gentle! Sitting in the waiting room you could hear the drone of the drill as the poor unfortunate in the dentist's chair was having his teeth attended to. Apprehensively, I would go in to Mr Lamb's surgery and sit in the big brown leather chair, which tilted back slightly. The main worry was the drill. There were no local anaesthetic injections when you had a filling; just straight in with the whirring instrument of torture. By today's standards the drill was very slow and extremely noisy. I think it was electric but I also have a vague memory of a pedal powered drill. It wasn't very efficient and the noise as the drill bit in to the tooth enamel was almost as bad as the inevitable stab of pain as Mr Lamb apologised for hitting another nerve.

Text D: Can we live without modern technology?

Could your family 'unplug' for a week? Robert Crampton talks about how he and his family unplugged for a week and lived without modern technology.

Most families and households have smartphones, laptops, tablets and family members are forever emailing, texting, tweeting and checking the internet or social media.

The Cramptons decided to take it back to 1980 before all these things were in use and they found their family experiment tough going.

Robert Crampton says: 'I didn't think it would be easy. But I didn't think it would be so difficult either. Certainly, I didn't imagine it would prove nigh on impossible … We only had to do it for a week. Seven days, I reasoned, should not be too hard. Right.'

They unplugged and hid laptops, mobiles, Sky, computer consoles and all other gadgets and gizmos.

Instead they imagined they would 'all sit around the fire and, um, read poetry. Or embroider stuff. Or something. It'd be fine.'

In fact it was, he says 'a farce'.

One of the first hurdles was letting their 12 year old go out without being able to phone or text to let her parents know she was OK. 'The truth is, the thought of my daughter going out at night without her mobile is as horrifying to me as it is to her … Has technology made my generation more protective, more controlling, of our children than our parents were of us? Undoubtedly, yes.'

He replaced his son's iPod with a clunky Sony walkman and some mix tapes. Then he introduced him to the delights of Owzthat – a cricket game from the '80s which his son declared 'tragic'!

And as for the parents they found themselves so addicted to their computers, tablets and smart phones that neither of them lasted past day three.

Even TV not being in on demand was tough: 'Having to watch TV in the traditional fashion is dire. I watch a fair number of TV programmes, but hardly any of them, not for several years, as part of the normal schedule. The screen seemed a ridiculously long way away. I'd forgotten how appalling adverts are.'

Being tied to a landline with a curly wire was also frustrating: 'I'm used to being able to make a call and move around doing other stuff – tidying up the kitchen, sorting out the bottles and papers for recycling, that sort of thing. To have to sit in one place was frustrating. Beyond frustrating, actually. Unnatural. Wasteful. I kept the phone thing going for four whole days – then binned it.'

His conclusion:

'Throughout this experiment, I didn't feel any such benefit. I felt bored, unconnected, limited, out of touch – and, if not exactly powerless, then certainly much more beholden to the decisions of others. I felt, in other words, remarkably similar to how I felt growing up in a provincial suburb in the Seventies. Why would I want to feel like that all over again? Once was enough. And why would I want to inflict it on my children?'

www.thetimes.co.uk

Activity 6

1 **Read Text A.** What are the two main opinions in the text?

2 How reliable is the information in the text? Give reasons for your view.

3 **Read Text B.** Which of the following statements is false?
   a   The text uses lots of statistics.
   b   The text is an example of a non-continuous text.
   c   The text uses quotes from people involved.
   d   The text is written in an impersonal style.

4 A student has made the following statements about Text B. Think about whether the statements are reliable or not and why.
   a   The writer is concerned about missing nuclear weapons.
   b   The text uses a non-emotive tone.
   c   There is a desire in the world to reduce the number of nuclear weapons stockpiled.
   d   The writer is 100 per cent sure that the information in the text is accurate.
   e   The map and the table present the same information in different forms.

Activity 7

1 **Look at Text C.** What do you think the writer feels about how technology has progressed in the field of healthcare? Support your ideas with references to the text.

2 **Look at Text D.** Select **three** unsupported statements from the article.

3 What arguments does the article make in favour of modern technologies?

Test yourself

What **impressions** do you get of Robert Crampton and his family? **How** are these impressions created? [10]

Support your points with references from the text.

What I think	Evidence
They are quite well off.	They have a lot of technology such as 'laptops, mobiles, Sky, computer consoles'.
	'... his son declared "tragic"!'
They seem quite confident at first.	

Top tips

For the impressions Test yourself question, it is important to find a **range** of different points. The second part of the question needs to address 'how' with references to the text. It may help to think of a table like the one below. Some ideas have been filled in to start you off.

Writing

Learning objectives

In this unit you will be:
- writing clearly and effectively;
- adapting your style to suit purpose and audience – informal letter-writing;
- paragraphing and presenting work appropriately;
- developing expository and advisory writing.

Activity 8

Which of these features would you use in formal or informal letters? Or both? Complete a Venn diagram to put them into each category.

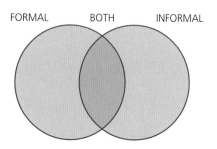

full address   *shortened address*   *paragraphs*   *second person*

subheadings   *friendly tone*   *exclamations*   *first person*

text speak   *statistics*   *formal register*   *abbreviations*

quotes   *expert opinion*   *lively style*   *opinions*

third person   *humour*

Stretch

Add other appropriate features to your Venn diagram.

Activity 9

What does it mean to **advise** someone? What examples can you think of in life where someone might advise someone else? Make a list and be prepared to share your ideas with the class.

Activity 10

When advising someone, what do you consider important? Below are some ideas that might be considered important when advising. Use the second and third columns to write an explanation and example of what you think is meant by each device.

Devices to use when advising	Your explanation of the term	Example
Informal language		
Opinions		
Anecdotes		
Supporting evidence		
Using the second person for direct address		
Giving specific, tailored advice		
Using humour		
Giving different options		
Using imperatives or directions		

Activity 11 Editorial skills

Read the paragraph below from a letter of advice to a friend who has asked whether he should complete his driving test. Then answer the questions that follow.

Driving has made a huge difference to my life! I think I would go mad if I didn't have the freedom of my car! There are lots of respectable driving schools around that you can use. I went with 'Carmen's Cars' and found them to be patient and reliable. Other reputable companies I know of include 'Dave's Driving School' and 'Round the Bend'.

Driving is so ....(1).... in today's world that if you don't drive, there's every chance you'll be .....(2)..... from your friends and family. ....(3)....., you'll be able to run errands for your grandparents and ease the ....(4)..... on your mum and dad.

1 Circle the word which best fits the gap:

   1 famous   small   essential   everywhere

   2 annoyed   independent   isolated   alone

   3 Additionally   Conversely   However   Stubbornly

   4 worries   burden   eyebrows   amount

2 How many of the devices from Activity 10 can you find in the paragraphs?

Activity 12 Put it to the proof

The following excerpt from an informal letter was written to someone's Great Aunt advising whether she should get a digital radio. As she is a bit of a stickler for correct spelling, punctuation and grammar, the writer has asked you to check it! There are at least ten mistakes to find and correct.

Digital radioes have much clearer sound than an ordinary radio Often with an older stile radio, you gets a lot of background noise and humming, but with a digital radio the noise is sharp, crisp, and clear. I now you like lisening to the archers on radio 4, well you will hear the farm animals very clearly! Not only this but digital radioes look a lot smarter than ordinary radios. There is a huge range of colors and designs and you will be able to get one that matches your house. My mother brought one that complimented her kitchen blind and it looks so smart!

What errors did you spot? Identify these as Spelling, Punctuation or Grammar errors below.

Spelling	Punctuation	Grammar
e.g. radioes	e.g. no full stop	e.g. expression errors

Stretch

Expand the letter to include the remaining elements.

Stretch

What features of writing to advise have been included in the extract for Activity 12? What extra features could be included?

Test yourself

Read the following exam-style question carefully:

> An elderly relative asks for your advice and opinion about the benefits of getting a new laptop. Write a letter, giving them advice on this purchase and explaining what the benefits might be for them and their family. [35]

Think about:

- the age and possible interests of the recipient and how the internet may be of help in areas of his/her life;
- the format of your letter;
- the style, vocabulary and techniques you may use.

Planning your answer

Before starting (as with any extended writing task) it is important to PLAN your response. In the exam you will be given 10 minutes to plan your answer, and this will help you write a more sustained response. Think of four or five areas that you want to cover. Each 'area' can be turned into a heading or topic sentence starter. For example:

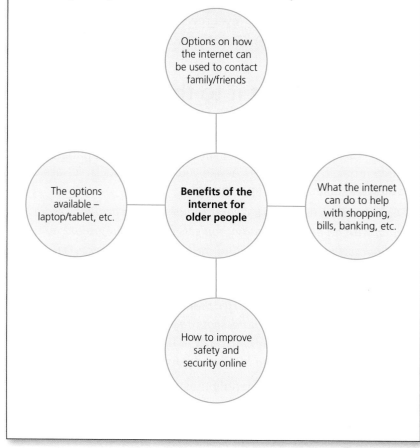

Varying sentence structures

In an informal letter (as in any piece of extended writing), it is important to vary and use a range of sentence structures.

When you have written your response to the question, use the checklist below to make sure you have used a variety of sentences.

Here are some points to consider. Have I:

	Yes	No
Used short sentences for clarity and impact?		
Used longer sentences for more balanced statements and follow up sentences?		
Been aware of the 'comma splice'? When sentences run on for too long they become difficult to follow. Check whether you need a full stop instead of a comma.		
Avoided expanding sentences by overusing 'and' or 'but'.		
Varied the starts of sentences. Try beginning sentences with words ending with '-ly', '-ed' and '-ing'.		

Top tips

Format: the layout of an informal letter is less important than a formal letter. However, you would be expected to include a date, brief address, suitable opening ('Dear Jemma'), paragraphs, (including introduction and conclusion) and appropriate signing off.

3c Into the future

Oracy

Activity 1

Look at the following inventions:

Sweep shoes

These shoes can be used to sweep up without bending over. One shoe is a brush and the other is a dust pan.

Butter stick

To smear butter on toast, simply smear it using this butter stick. Easy to use, like a glue stick.

Slow melting ice cream

Ice cream that will not melt away on a summer's day. A new protein in the ice cream has the benefit of locking in cold temperatures, meaning that the ice cream stays cold for longer.

360 degree dog washer

A ring-shaped dog shower that lets you bathe your dog by simply moving the hoop along the length of their body.

Flask sandals

These shoes have an in-built liquid storage, allowing you to have access to drinks while on the go, without cumbersome flasks.

- Discuss the advantages that each product offers.
- Discuss the drawbacks and disadvantages that each product might have.
- As a group, rank order them in terms of how successful they are likely to be in the marketplace.

The table below may help you to shape your discussion.

Name of product	Advantages	Disadvantages
Sweep shoes		

Stretch

Think of a new name and slogan for each invention. Try to make use of alliteration, onomatopoeia, pun or rhyme for each of the slogans.

Write a brief pitch for your favourite invention.

Activity 2

Using what you found out in Activity 1, summarise **three** issues designers need to take into account when launching a new product.

Activity 3

Discuss the following 'irritations' and think about an idea for an invention that would help.
- Getting ready for school in the morning.
- Using your phone – texting or speaking.
- Food – what irritates you about certain foods, or the way they are served or prepared?
- Car journeys – what do you hate about this?
- Pets and animals – how might we improve their lives?
- Shopping – how might this experience be improved?
- A new sport – maybe an amalgamation of two or more current ones.
- Chores! How can we make chores more interesting?
- An invention to improve the world!

Activity 4

In pairs, create an invention of your own. For your product you will need to create:
- a description of the product and explanation of how you decided on it;
- a brand name and slogan for the product;
- an outline of the product which includes cost of materials;
- an explanation of costs and profits, plus the audience you are aiming for.

Activity 5

As part of a larger group, you will have to explain and 'pitch' your product to other students in the class.

Top tips

Anticipate the questions you may receive from investors. Think about the questions you can ask others and that you may be asked. Here are some question starters to get you going, but you can think of others:

What are the advantages of …?

What are the disadvantages of …?

Why is it necessary to …?

What do you think of …?

What might children think of …?

Reading

Learning objectives

In this unit you will be:
- retrieving and analysing information;
- synthesising information;
- interpreting themes and ideas;
- improving your editing skills.

Text A: Extract from a 1967 issue of 'The Futurist' magazine where Hubert H. Humphrey, the Vice President of the United States, wrote a piece stating his vision of the future

Here are some of the developments we can look forward to within the next 20 years:

In agriculture, the large-scale use of de-salinated sea water.

In medicine, the transplantation of natural organs and the use of artificial ones.

In psychiatry, the widespread application of drugs that control or modify the personality.

In education, the use of more sophisticated teaching machines.

In wordwide communication, the everyday employment of translating machines.

In industry, the extensive use of automation, up to and including some kinds of decision-making at the management level.

In space, the establishment of a permanent base upon the moon.

For the year 2000, however, we can foresee some really far-out developments:

The virtual elimination of bacterial and viral diseases.

The correction of hereditary defects through the modification of genetic chemistry.

The stepping-up of our food supply through large-scale ocean-farming and fabrication of synthetic proteins.

Control of the weather, at least on a regional scale.

In space, the landing of men on Mars and the establishment of a permanent unmanned research station on that planet.

The creation, in the laboratory, of primitive forms of artificial life.

Activity 6

1 Look at Text A. Read the following quote:

'In medicine, the transplantation of natural organs and the use of artificial ones.'

What word could replace 'transplantation' in this sentence without affecting its meaning?
a replacement
b transportation
c replace
d trialling

2 In your opinion, what are the three most positive 'developments' from the list of predictions for the year 2000? Explain your ideas with clear reasons for your choices.

Top tips

Try substituting each word in the sentence and reading it aloud.

Text B: Extract from an internet article, 'The 10 Dangers Posed By Future Technology'

The total loss of privacy

There are plenty of people who would argue that this isn't a problem posed by future technology, but one which is already here. After the recent revelations that a range of new smart TVs may be recording users' private conversations and sharing the details with third parties, the fear that our home appliances may be spying on us is becoming less sci-fi paranoia and more a real concern.

So where will this end? Will the rush to embrace the digital era mean us waving goodbye to our privacy forever? The worry is that a day may come where every single aspect of our lives is monitored and recorded by governments who want to know what we're up to, conglomerates investigating our spending habits, or even banks making sure we aren't living above our means.

The often repeated line from those wishing to take our privacy away from us is that it is for our own protection. That if we're so concerned about our privacy, then we must have something to hide; so stop closing the bathroom door when you go to the toilet, it makes you look suspicious.

Having a totally machine based workforce

Advancements in technology have always posed the risk of creating machines that do the jobs of humans. Manufacturing jobs in particular are often one of the most at risk areas.

Previous employment areas which were once considered 'human only' are now being taken over by machines. Twenty years ago a self-checkout machine was thought impossible, now there are almost half a million worldwide, enabling one member of staff to run up to six checkout lanes at a time.

With AI becoming ever more advanced, there may come a time when computers are able to do jobs which require human decision making. With automatic cars also just around the corner, will the sole job for humans in the future be the repair and maintenance of the machines which took their jobs? Or at least until a device is invented that can do that as well.

The death of human interaction

Another future danger which many claim is a problem we are facing today. Has the advent of social media made society anything but social? Would you prefer to purchase something online or using a machine rather than talk to a fellow human being? Is texting always better than speaking over the phone? The accusations of technology destroying the art of conversation may hold some truth, but what of the future? How will the next generation's children of the digital age interact with others?

The over-reliance on technology

While technology undoubtedly has the ability to advance us as humans, becoming over-reliant on it may actually reduce our intelligence. There are numerous examples today of drivers blindly following GPS instructions into rivers and ditches, people who cannot spell without the use of a word processor, and those who cannot perform simple math problems without the use of a calculator.

So what will the future give us? Top scientist Professor Stephen Hawking said, 'The development of full artificial intelligence could spell the end of the human race.'

Eventually the human race may lose the skills it has gained over the years, with almost every aspect of our lives totally reliant on technology. The problem will come if that technology ever fails, or turns against us.

http://csglobe.com

Activity 7 Editorial skills

Read these extra paragraphs from Text B on page 95 then answer the questions that follow:

The increase in technology-related illnesses

There have been few _____(1)_____ as controversial as the link between human illness, _____(2)_____ cancer, and modern technology.

1 Choose the word below that best fits gap (1):
   a wonders
   b issues
   c decisions
   d explanations

2 Choose the word below that best fits gap (2):
   a allege
   b allegedly
   c specific
   d specifically

While the _____(1)_____ amount of evidence suggests that the use of cell phones and wi-fi does not increase the risk of cancer, there have been some studies _____(2)_____ the opposite is true.

3 Choose the pair of words that best fit the meaning of the sentence above:
   a majority … when
   b most … making
   c overwhelming … suggesting
   d latest … stating
   e minority … conclusively

4 'The writer of Text B has a very negative view of future technology.' Find five pieces of evidence to support this statement and explain **how** they support the statement.

Activity 8

Look at Text B on page 95 **and** Text C below. **Synthesise** what the texts suggest are the advantages and disadvantages of the increased use of machines.

Use the table below to help plan your answer.

Advantages		Disadvantages	
Text B	Text C	Text B	Text C

Top tips

Synthesise means that *you do not have to compare* across both texts. Rather than look at each text separately, it may be better to make the focus of the question drive your underlining. Look for advantages across **both** texts before tackling the disadvantages.

Text C: Extract from 'I, Robot' by Isaac Asimov (Harper Voyager, 2013). In this extract, the robot QT (Cutie) reflects on the difference between robots and humans

Cutie laughed. It was a very inhuman laugh – the most machine-like utterance he had yet given vent to. It was sharp and explosive, as regular as a metronome and as uninflected.

'Look at you,' he said finally. 'I say this in no spirit of contempt, but look at you! The material you are made of is soft and flabby, lacking endurance and strength, depending for energy upon the inefficient oxidation of organic material – like that.' He pointed a disapproving finger at what remained of Donovan's sandwich. 'Periodically you pass into a coma and the least variation in temperature, air pressure, humidity, or radiation intensity impairs your efficiency. You are makeshift.

'I, on the other hand, am a finished product. I absorb electrical energy directly and utilize it with an almost one hundred percent efficiency. I am composed of strong metal, am continuously conscious, and can stand extremes of environment easily. These are facts which, with the self-evident proposition that no being can create another being superior to itself, smashes your silly hypothesis to nothing.'

Text D: Extract from the novel, 'The Time Machine' by H.G. Wells (William Heinemann, 1895). In this extract, the time traveller describes an encounter with Morlocks, a branch of future mankind, in their underground world

They started away, and then I could feel them approaching me again. They clutched at me more boldly, whispering odd sounds to each other. I shivered violently, and shouted again—rather discordantly. This time they were not so seriously alarmed, and they made a queer laughing noise as they came back at me. I will confess I was horribly frightened. I determined to strike another match and escape under the protection of its glare. I did so, and eking out the flicker with a scrap of paper from my pocket, I made good my retreat to the narrow tunnel. But I had scarce entered this when my light was blown out and in the blackness I could hear the Morlocks rustling like wind among leaves, and pattering like the rain, as they hurried after me.

In a moment I was clutched by several hands, and there was no mistaking that they were trying to haul me back. I struck another light, and waved it in their dazzled faces. You can scarce imagine how nauseatingly inhuman they looked—those pale, chinless faces and great, lidless, pinkish-grey eyes!—as they stared in their blindness and bewilderment. But I did not stay to look, I promise you: I retreated again, and when my second match had ended, I struck my third. It had almost burned through when I reached the opening into the shaft. I lay down on the edge, for the throb of the great pump below made me giddy. Then I felt sideways for the projecting hooks, and, as I did so, my feet were grasped from behind, and I was violently tugged backward.

Top tips

1 Highlight the areas that are crucial to the question.
2 'What' refers to the situation and events happening which create tension.
3 'How' refers to the choices the writer has made in terms of vocabulary choices, sentence structures and any other methods used.

Activity 9

1 Look at Text D. How does the writer create tension and excitement in this extract? Think of **what** he says and **how** he says it.
2 Look at the table below – two of the quotes are not 'well-chosen'. Can you identify these and replace them with two more appropriate quotations?

Evidence	How is tension and excitement created?
This time they were not so seriously alarmed	
I was horribly frightened	
They hurried after me	
I made good my retreat	
I was violently tugged backwards	

Writing

Activity 10

Read the following two student responses to the following question:

Describe an occasion when someone unexpectedly comes into some money.

- Discuss which is most effective with a learning partner.
- Outline three ways each writer has tried to engage the reader.

Sample student responses

Student A

The boy sat on the cracked, plastic seat of the bus shelter. His shoulders sagged and he felt the heavy weight of his head pulling his whole body forward as sleep battled to take hold. The crush of people around him only served to provide warmth and the chatter of many in the crowd was a lullaby: enticing him to sleep.

Suddenly, the boy was awake. The shelter felt different: cold and unwelcoming. He suddenly noticed the acrid stench of urine that pervaded the shelter. With a groan, he heaved himself off the hard, plastic ridged seat and as he did so, his foot knocked against a plain brown envelope. The boy's heart raced as he gingerly bent over to pick it up. His numb fingers could barely prize apart the paper, but when he did so, a flash of green illuminated his face. Five pound notes. Wads of them. He whistled involuntarily.

Student B

My mum was watching TV. She had her lottery ticket in her lap. She was excited as the numbers rolled out of the machine.

4 – 23 – 14 – 17 -39 – 62.

'Oh my god!' she shouted! 'I've won! I've won!' She was so excited that I thought her head would burst.

Now we live in a huge house with 6 bedrooms and 4 bathrooms and we have everything we want.

Activity 11

Read the following advice about good descriptive writing from a teacher's 'Good Practice' guide.

In each case, write what you think each piece of advice means. Can you spot these elements in the two student responses in Activity 10?

1 Keep the writing detailed ('zoomed in').
2 Keep the writing realistic.
3 Make sure what you write makes sense.
4 Write in complete sentences.
5 Include snippets of dialogue, if appropriate.

Activity 12

Similarly, the exam board highlights common mistakes that students make when writing descriptively.

Match the advice (A–F) to the example (1–6).

Advice	Example
A 'Overblown' writing	1 All I could see were the bright lights. I could hear loud music. I could smell delicious hot dogs and onions.
B Inappropriate or inaccurate vocabulary	2 The hectic, buzzing and lively playground was vibrantly and ecstatically alive with the spirited screams of excited and screechy children.
C Verbless sentence	3 The shouting of teenagers. The screams of girls. Adults trying to keep control.
D Unrealistic and inappropriate details	4 The delicious stench from the canteen drifted over my salivating nostrils.
E Generalisation	5 All the mothers were chatting as they waited for the children to emerge through the school gates.
F Overreliance on the senses as a 'formula' for writing	6 The playground was suddenly overrun with zombies. They chased the terrified children around the confined space, hungry for flesh.

Remember, writing to describe will involve more than just describing a scene. You should also consider expressing your thoughts, describing actions and recalling events.

Stretch

Choose three of these examples and try to improve them by using some of the features recommended for descriptive writing.

Activity 13 Put it to the proof

Correct this student's piece of descriptive writing about their favourite possession. There are ten errors in total.

My most valuble possession is an old slightly battered teddy bear – the first toy I were given. Hes nothing fancy, just an ordinary, brown bear, scuffed and tatty and well-loved. His fir is weared down by years of little fingers stroking, bashing and cramming into small spaces. He may not be totaly perfect but he still gave me comfort and reminds me of being a child, for that i will always treasure him.

What errors did you spot? Identify these as Spelling, Punctuation or Grammar errors below.

Spelling	Punctuation	Grammar
e.g. totaly	e.g. no apostrophe	e.g. expression errors

Stretch

This is a very short description. What advice would you give this student to **extend** their description?

Test yourself

Read the following exam-style questions carefully:

Describe seeing a new invention or toy for the first time.

Or

You have invented a new machine that can transport you into the future. Describe what happens when you step into this 'future' land. [35]

Think about:

- **planning** your description – what things can you describe;
- your **feelings** about the object or event;
- how it **changed** your view or outlook;
- concluding on what it means to you **now**.

Writing to **describe** will involve more than describing a scene. You should also consider expressing your thoughts, describing actions and recalling events.

Sample student responses

Read the following openings to the task:

Describe an incident that happened in a supermarket.

Match up the student response with the comments from the examiner on the next page. What advice would you give to the piece in most need of improvement?

N.B. The sample answers on the next page do not represent full responses. A full response should be 350–500 words long.

Student A

Unable to face the queue of dreary shoppers (particularly the mother with a towering trolley and crying baby) I knew the time had come. I had to face the self service till. An impatient shop assistant pointed gormlessly to the vacant machine and I smiled my thanks before heading over to the mechanical menace.

'How many bags are you using?' was the first of a series of questions.

This seemed innocuous enough. None. (I only had a dry looking sandwich and an overpriced bottle of orange juice.) I punched the '0' button.

I breathed a sigh of relief. This was going well. I was gaining in confidence.

'Please scan your first item.'

I passed my sandwiches in front of the laser beam and heard the satisfying beep.

'Please place the item in the bagging area.'

The monotonous, overly friendly drone was starting to grate on my nerves. Nevertheless, I complied and put my egg and cress delight on the silver plated surface.

'Unexpected item in baggage area.' I was sure I could hear a tone of satisfaction in the electronic voice.

I swore under my breath. It had all been going so well.

Student B

The till was glowing in the dark supermarket. It looked evil, like a robot from Doctor Who. I stepped casually in front of it and it asked me to scan my goods. I did this and there was a high pitched beep. I put the item in my bag and fed my coins into the slot. I heard them fall with a clunk and I was reminded of the arcade at the seaside.

Student C

I seen the machine was a screen at eye level and a scanner below. The screen was glossy and reminded me of a computer screen I herd an electronic voice ask me to scan my item. I swung it in front and heard the beep. i put it in the bag.

Examiner comment 1:

While there are some effective words and phrases used in this piece, there is an uneasy sense of place that does not quite seem realistic. There are some odd vocabulary choices and the language is not always well-chosen.

Examiner comment 2:

This piece really engages the reader with a strong sense of place and audience. The student uses a range of ambitious vocabulary. There is a realism about the writing but slightly heightened for comic effect – this is done deliberately and with purpose.

Examiner comment 3:

This is quite a straightforward extract. There is some attempt to describe but this is quite underdeveloped. There are some basic spelling and grammar issues.

Unit 4: The world of work

4a   A man's world?

Oracy

Learning objectives

In this unit you will be:
- interacting with others;
- drawing ideas together;
- presenting ideas clearly;
- responding to others' questions.

Activity 1

Enter the Dragon's Den …

In the previous unit you created a new product which you pitched to a group of students. Now you will make a sales pitch to 'sell' your product to 'the Dragons'.

This task will test your ability to **argue** your point of view and **persuade** the 'Dragons' to fund your project using your Oracy skills.

Look at the pitch below from a successful entrepreneur. Copy and complete the table following the extract.

Hi, I'm Kirsty. I'm 24 years old and I'm here today asking for £65,000 for a 15 per cent equity stake in my company, Worthenshaws. Worthenshaws produce healthy and innovative alternatives to ice cream. We currently have two brands on the market and five different products. All our products are low in fat and low in calories and are free from dairy, sugar, gluten, artificial additives, soya, cholesterol and nuts. My first product is called Cocounuka.

Coconuka contains active Manuka honey, Echinacea, from New Zealand. It's ideal for sore throats, coughs and colds. My second range is Coconice. These are in three flavours: chocolate, strawberry and vanilla. The inspiration behind my range stems from my four-year-old child who has a serious nut allergy and is dairy intolerant. I began selling them four months ago nationally via a health distribution company in the UK. I spoke to a number of large retailers and I've gained a considerable amount of interest. I'd also like to, oh basically, I'd like to use your investment to help raise brand awareness with marketing and PR and also buy stock. Thank you.

Here are some techniques you might consider when writing your pitch:

Feature	Example
First person pronoun 'I' or 'we'	
Use of more complex vocabulary	
Use of subject-specific words and business language, e.g. units, equity	
Statistics to support your ideas	
Real-life experience (anecdote) to support your case	

Stretch

Can you find two or three other features to include?

Activity 2

The entrepreneur above has worked from bullet points of **key ideas** rather than reading from a complete script. These are the first of her bullet points – can you fill in the rest of her bullet points by looking at the extract above?

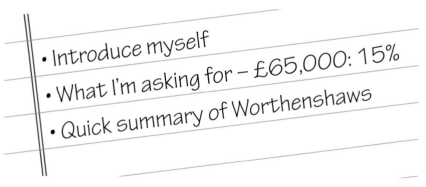

- Introduce myself
- What I'm asking for – £65,000: 15%
- Quick summary of Worthenshaws

Activity 3

Now write your own pitch, and then reduce it to a series of bullet points to help you with the real thing.

Then pitch it!

Top tips

In your presentation, remember to explain:
1 The purpose of presentation – mention the brand name.
2 Where your ideas have come from.
3 The benefits that the product could bring – what would inspire people to buy it?
4 The cost and estimated profits the product will make.
5 Who the product is aimed at and how you would aim to sell it.

Prepare for difficult questions from other students after delivering your pitch.

Activity 4

Questioning is going to be important to find out more about the pitch. Open questions are particularly good at getting 'pitchers' to open up (and make mistakes!). Look at the questions below and discuss how effective they are at getting entrepreneurs to 'open up':

1 What inspired you to create this product?

2 How much profit will you make?

3 Why do you think the product will be successful?

4 How will you spend my investment money?

5 How much does one of those cost?

> **Stretch**
>
> Advanced questioning:
>
> - Show confidence by starting with an imperative rather than a question, e.g. 'Tell me about …'
> - Show reflective questioning skills by 'echoing' a point made in the pitch and then a follow-up, e.g. 'You just said you will make £100,000 profit in the first year. What evidence have you got for this?'
>
> Try to incorporate this style of questioning for the Q and A part of the pitch.

Top tips

Closed questions invite short, focused answers, e.g. 'When did you arrive?', 'Do you like chips?'

Open questions invite longer responses, e.g. 'Why did you think of that?', 'How do you feel about…?'

There is nothing wrong with closed questions as a starting point, but try to follow these with an open question.

Can you think of follow-up open questions for the two closed questions opposite (questions 2 and 5)?

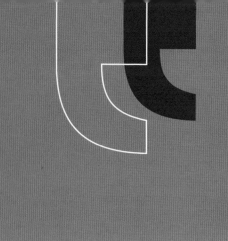

Reading

Learning objectives

In this unit you will be:
- retrieving and synthesising information;
- supporting your ideas with appropriate evidence;
- making inferences in texts.

Activity 5

Read through these extracts and then answer the questions below.

Text A: Which professions have more women than men?

The majority of journalists, authors, teachers, lab technicians, editors and public relations officers are women. It could be argued that women now hold the majority of so-called professional jobs in Britain. Since it is International Women's Day, perhaps we should celebrate the recent strides that have been made in striving for equality for women in the job market.

However, only 22% of MPs and peers are women and a similar percentage of women are judges.

Sadly, statistics confirm that there are 13.58 million men working full time compared to 7.68 million women. This would follow that men make up 58% of the workforce compared to 42% women. Women will undoubtedly still suffer from glass ceilings in their professional and public lives in some parts of the country.

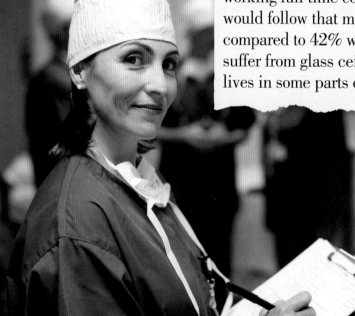

Text B: Number of women in work in Britain hits record high – but figures show the gender pay gap is growing too ('The Independent')

More women are in work than ever before as official figures show a record-breaking 14 million now have jobs. The female employment rate reached 67.2 per cent last year, the highest since the Office for National Statistics' records began.

However, experts cautioned today that this rise had coincided with an increase in the gender pay gap, as median wages for women fell. The increase was also largely created by more women declaring themselves self-employed, which could mean many pocketing paltry sums far below the minimum wage.

Overall, 193,000 more men and women got jobs between October and December 2013, taking the total number in work to 30.15 million people. British workers made up almost nine-tenths of the employment rise.

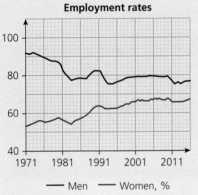

Employment rates

—— Men —— Women, %

Source: ONS

Diane Elson, Chair of the UK Women's Budget Group, which analyses how women fare in the labour market, told *The Independent*: 'While it's good to see women's employment rate increasing, we have to look at the quality of employment. There are two things in the latest statistics that the Government is not highlighting: median wages and self-employment.

The median weekly earnings for men rose from £502 to £508 over the last year, but for women they fell from £413 to £411. This means the gender pay gap has now risen from £89 to £97 a week.

Much of the rise in employment amongst women was down to more declaring themselves self-employed. Professor Elson believes that this category could hide large numbers putting in very long hours for little financial return.

www.independent.co.uk, 19 Feb 2014

Text C: Women's jobs in the 20th century, by Tim Lambert

More occupations were opened to women in the 20th century. In 1910 the first policewoman was appointed in Los Angeles. In 1916 the first policewoman (with full powers) was appointed in Britain. The 1919 Sex Disqualification Removal Act allowed women to become lawyers, vets and civil servants. (The first woman solicitor in Britain was Carrie Morrison in 1922). Also in 1922 Irene Barclay became the first British woman chartered surveyor. In 1958 Hilda Harding became the first woman bank manager in Britain. In 1976 Mary Langdon became the first woman firefighter in Britain.

Nevertheless in the early 20th century it was unusual for married women to work (except in wartime). However in the 1950s and 1960s it became common for them to do so – at least part-time. New technology in the home made it easier for women to do paid work. Before the 20th century housework was so time-consuming married women did not have time to work. At the same time the economy changed. Manufacturing became less important and service industries grew, creating more opportunities for women.

Technological and economic changes made it inevitable that women would be given the same rights as men. In the USA in 1963 the Equal Pay Act was passed. It compelled employers to pay men and women equal pay for equal work. In the UK in 1970 a similar act was passed. In 1975 the Sex Discrimination Act was passed in Britain. It made it illegal to discriminate against women in employment, education and training. In 1984 a new law in Britain stated that equal pay must be given for work of equal value.

www.localhistories.org

Text D: Careers Brits think men and women shouldn't do

One of the key objectives of the survey was to understand if there is still a divide in public opinion on whether or not men and women are equally well-suited for various jobs. Here is how people in the study answered the questions about occupations that may be traditionally viewed as more male or female:

Which gender are better at the following professions?

The results demonstrate a clear divide, with over 60% of people saying men make better electricians, plumbers and mechanics, and 50% saying men are better pilots.

76% of the survey respondees said women make better nannies, florists and nurses.

To gain a greater understanding of these sexist attitudes, the study also considered the extent to which people believe certain jobs are suitable, or indeed, unsuitable for a man or a woman.

Their responses revealed a worrying degree of sexism, with 24 to 26% of all participants saying that men simply should not pursue a career as a beautician, a midwife or a nanny.

In addition, between 19 to 22% of people think women should steer clear of jobs such as security guard, refuse collector or soldier. 15% think women should not be mechanics, and 13% say women should steer clear of a career in plumbing.

www.worldplayzinc.com

1 Read Text A and decide to what extent you agree with the statements:
   a 'Women have now achieved greater equality with men.'
   b 'Men are generally in higher paid jobs than women.'
   Support your ideas with evidence from the text.

2 Text A uses the sentence, 'Women will undoubtedly still suffer from glass ceilings...'. Select one definition from the list below that best explains the sentence:
   a Women can see through the weaknesses in an organisation.
   b There is a barrier preventing from women advancing in their career.
   c Women do not like being in dark rooms.
   d Some women have modern, open-plan offices.

3 Read Text B and look at the two statements for 1a and 1b again. What extra evidence have you found to support or refute these statements?

4 This text uses the phrase, 'the gender pay gap'. Explain what this phrase means in your own words.

5 Read Text C. Explain why women's job opportunities improved in the twentieth century.

6 According to Text D, what evidence is given to show 'a worrying degree of sexism' in people's attitudes to work?

7 Now look across ALL the texts on the page and **synthesise** all the evidence that supports the statement, 'there is a worrying degree of sexism in attitudes to work'.

Activity 6

Read the extract on the facing page and then answer the questions that follow.

Time for a reality check

Karren Brady, the star of 'The Apprentice' has enjoyed huge success in business and a high media profile since becoming the MD of Birmingham City FC at the age of 23.

When Brady joined the league of WAGS (she married Canadian-born and then Birmingham City striker, Paul Peschisolido in 1995 and has two children with him) she was managing director of Birmingham City football club. This is a role she took on at the tender age of 23. It made her headline news, as both her youth and gender was extraordinary in the world of football.

Turning loss into profit

Despite her youth and lack of knowledge of the football business, Brady succeeded in turning around the fortunes of Birmingham. When she started at the club it was in administration but by the end of her first year it had made a trading profit. Within just a few years the club made an overall profit for the first time, and in 1997 it floated on the stock market, valued at the time at £25 million.

During her tenure at Birmingham the average gate rose from 6,000 to more than 30,000 and in 2009 it was sold for £82m. It was a rare beast in premiership football – a debt-free, profit-making football club.

Perhaps Brady's success is down to her non-fanlike attitude to the game. Football is a business like any other to Brady, although with its own unique set of circumstances.

A man's world?

Building brands, even in the precarious world of football, has become a central tenet of Brady's approach and she appears to have adopted that same philosophy as an individual, ensuring that her profile is maintained and building her personal brand. As a no-nonsense, straight-talking, thick-skinned football exec she carved out a niche as a high-profile businesswoman succeeding in a male-dominated industry. High-profile women in business have often built a career in more obviously female-friendly environments, so those that do it in more masculine industries stand out from the crowd.

However, Brady queries the perception that football is male-dominated. 'Football may appear to be very

male-dominated but actually there are an awful lot of women who work in football. I'm a passionate believer in promoting women in business, and when I left Birmingham 75 per cent of the senior management team at director level were women. So it appears to be male-dominated but when you get behind the scenes it isn't. And it's a great business, it's a people business which suits my skills,' she says.

You're hired!

Brady's career has always been followed by a flurry of media attention, which she seems more than happy to have courted. The impressive boardroom performances have gone hand-in-hand with TV show appearances, *Hello!* magazine photo spreads and book writing. So when it was announced last year that Margaret Mountford was leaving *The Apprentice*, there was a degree of inevitability that Brady should replace her as Lord Sugar's female sidekick, despite her very different style. Brady had already familiarised herself with the format – albeit on the other side of the table – when she featured in the Comic Relief version of the show in 2006 and led the women's team to a resounding victory over the men. In many ways the show is perfect for Brady, combining her business and media acumen, so it is not surprising that she has been pleased to be part of it. 'Alan Sugar is fantastic; the integrity, the professionalism, the amount of hard work that goes into making that show is truly amazing,' she says.

But perhaps one of the most pertinent insights into Brady's business view comes when she's asked how she deals with her mistakes. 'It's always important to learn from your mistakes but it's far more important to learn from other people's successes.'

www.rbs.businesssense.co.uk

1 Read the section, 'Turning loss into profit'. How did Karren Brady succeed at Birmingham FC?
2 Look at the sections, 'A Man's World?' and 'You're Hired'. What impressions do you have of Karren Brady in these sections? How are these impressions created?

The table below selects some **appropriate** and **less appropriate** evidence from the text. Which evidence is most appropriate? Can you replace these with more well-chosen examples?

Evidence	What it suggests about Karren Brady
'lack of knowledge in the football business'	
'A man's world?'	
'no-nonsense, straight-talking'	
'thick-skinned'	
'High profile women have often built a career'	
'passionate'	
'impressive board-room performances'	

Stretch

Identify the partial quotations in the table. What other misunderstandings might be made by candidates when answering the question on Karren Brady above?

Top tips

Beware of using *partial quotations*. This refers to quotations that do not give the full picture and could be misleading. Look at the two comments based on the following:

When the multi-billionaire was quizzed about his interest in Formula 1 he told us: 'I'm hungry to succeed in this industry'.

1 'I'm hungry to succeed in this industry' suggests that someone is ambitious.
2 The entrepreneur is always 'hungry' which suggests he has a big appetite.

Which comment uses **partial quotation** and what are the dangers here?

Writing

Activity 7 Put it to the proof

The following leaflet has been written by Work This Way – an award-winning social and environmental business. The copy writer has been tasked with proofreading the leaflet before it is uploaded onto the website. Identify these errors in Spelling, Punctuation or Grammar (there are 10 in total) below.

Spelling	Punctuation	Grammar
e.g. interveiw	e.g. no full stop	e.g. expression errors

Job interviews

Read as much about the commpany as posible this shows you are enthusitic intrested and prepared to put in the effort.

Before the interview

Remind yourself of what the job intails. Think of positive examples from previous expierences that you could use if asked to illustrate why you would be good at the job.

- Think about questions you might be asked.
- Think of some questions you want to ask.
- Work out how you are going to explain about gaps in your CV and work history.

Be prepared for the interview

- Find out were it is.
- Leave plenty of time to get there.
- Check parking/transport.
- Take interveiw letter/portfolio/pen/notes.
- Take mobile/money in case you need to phone ahead.

Stretch

As a proofreader, what advice would you give this writer in order to improve his/her mechanical skills?

What spelling rules can you think of that might help improve accuracy?

Activity 8

Leaflets are usually written to **give information** and to **explain clearly** to a specific audience what you believe they need to know about a particular topic. Leaflets often have a **persuasive** tone.

Complete this mind map to help you think about the **audience** and **purpose** of a leaflet. Give some examples of different types of leaflets and where you might find them.

Activity 9

The following list contains features often found in leaflets. Copy the table below and arrange the features in three columns.

Layout	Content	Language

headline

a clear introduction

second person direct appeal

emotive/persuasive language

imperatives

first hand/personal experiences

addresses/helplines

subheadings

facts/statistics

expert opinions

helpful hints/advice

bullet points

pictures

logo

Top tips

Please note that the exam rubric is testing your writing skills only. What elements of your table are best avoided if you want to make best use of your time in the exam?

Activity 10

Read the text below, which is an extract from a leaflet. What is the purpose of this text? Is it:

- public
- personal
- educational
- occupational?

Give reasons for your choice.

> **We Are the Royal Navy**
>
> **You'll Protect the Nation's Interests. You'll Go Places**
>
> **This is life without limits**
>
> The incredible technology. The bond with colleagues. The amazing places. The doors that open. The difference you make to your nation – and the world.
>
> The Royal Navy means all these things and more. A life without limits is closer than you think.
>
> Seize it.
>
> You'd be forgiven for forgetting that Britain is an island nation. The clothes, food and petrol you depend on, in turn depend on the sea. Our whole economy, in fact, depends on shipping lanes that we keep open. It depends on the illegal activities that we disrupt, like piracy, drug and human trafficking – and the conflict that we prevent.
>
> We don't forget. We know that as long as it's business as usual for you, it's a job well done for us.
>
> *Everyday provides a different challenge. Hunting submarines or chasing drug-runners. It's not just a 9–5 job.*
>
> Tim, Warfare Specialist
>
> www.royalnavy.mod.uk/careers, www.royalnavy.mod.uk/brochure

Activity 11

Using a similar table to the one in Activity 9, spot all the language, content and layout features you noticed in the Royal Navy extract.

Test yourself

Read the following exam-style questions carefully:

Produce a leaflet explaining the product you created for your pitch at the start of this unit. This will help to bring the product to the marketplace.

Or

Produce a leaflet for a traditional 'male' industry (e.g. construction, the Army) which explains why females would find this a rewarding career. [35].

Top tips

While both of these leaflets may have a **persuasive** element, you will also have to **explain** the benefits and opportunities. This will require some **exposition** skills which rely on clear explanations and examples.

Planning your response

As with all the other extended writing tasks in this book, it is important to PLAN your response. This does not have to be too detailed but it will help you to organise your writing into sections.

It is always useful to think of the audience, purpose and format before you begin your answer. Aim to write two sides of A4. Remember that it is usually better not to write in columns, as it is difficult to work out whether you have written enough!

See the plan below for a leaflet explaining a new product, the *Woof-Washer*.

Complete an organised plan for your own leaflet.

Success criteria

Use the tables below to help self-assess your leaflet.

Communicate/Organise	Yes/No
Have I engaged the reader's interests with appropriate language features?	
Have I used the appropriate tone?	
Have I developed ideas fully?	
Does my leaflet have an appropriate layout and 'shape'?	

Accuracy	Yes/No
Have I varied my vocabulary?	
Have I used the right word choices?	
Have I varied my sentences?	
Have I checked my spelling and punctuation is correct?	
Have I checked my grammar and expression?	

Stretch

When you have completed the leaflet, go back and label all the features you have used.

4b Teenagers and work

Oracy

Activity 1

The headteacher of your school is considering stopping work experience in Year 11 to focus more intensively on exam preparation because students lose valuable teaching time. You have been asked for your opinion on whether work experience should remain for Y11 students.

Look at the following information and texts to help you form your argument.

Think about:
- what students hope to gain from work experience;
- the advantages and disadvantages of work experience.

Text 1

Over 95 per cent of students undertake work experience in Years 10 and 11. Most placements are arranged for the latter half of the summer term in Year 10 to avoid disruption to timetabled learning. Some placements last three weeks, but most finish after two weeks, or even one.

www.futuremorph

Text 2

Find a place that you know you will enjoy being at. I did my work experience last year and some of my friends and I have gone back to where we had our placement. This was because, firstly, we enjoyed being there and worked hard, and, secondly, because our work experience was successful and the company/shop liked us.

(Student blog)

Text 3

What young people need more than anything is work experience.

Most young people are really willing and able to dive into work, says Charlie Mayfield, chairman of the John Lewis Partnership. What they need more than anything is experience. Work experience means working, not making cups of tea. A little more planning by employers can make a big difference.

The Telegraph – Charlie Mayfield, 6/11/2012

Text 4

The Department for Education (DofE) definition of work experience is:
'A placement on employer's premises in which a student carries out a particular task or duty, or range of tasks or duties, more or less as would an employee, but with an emphasis on the learning aspects of the experience.'

Text 5

The benefits of work experience

When done well, work experience brings tangible benefits for young people, employer, schools and society as a whole. It can increase young people's confidence and promote social mobility by challenging stereotypes in relation to new career aspirations. Work experience can also bring the curriculum to life by showing how subjects can be applied and valued in the work place.

(Life Skills created with Barclays)

Text 7

My Year 11 students were involved in work experience for two weeks in September. They were taking their GCSE Maths exam 5 weeks later. This meant they missed out on six hours of essential teaching time just before this vital exam. In my opinion, work experience should be held at the end of Year 10 when it will not have such an impact on their learning!

(Maths teacher)

Text 6

I've done an awful lot better in my English, maths and science since I knew what I had to do to be an architect after the placement. I talked to one of the architects who told me what grades I needed and they were higher than I expected!

(Year 10 student)

Activity 2

In pairs, discuss your views on work experience.
Draw up a list of advantages and disadvantages for work experience. Rank order the most important benefits and drawbacks.

Activity 3

In groups of four, take on one of the following roles to come to a considered decision:

Your role is:	**Your role is**:
• a Year 11 student who feels work experience is worthwhile because it is helpful is making decisions about future career choices.	• a parent who is worried about the effect of missing lessons but can also see the benefits of experiencing a working environment.
Your role is:	**Your role is**:
• a headteacher who feels work experience is currently far too long and disrupts learning.	• an employer who has had problems with recent work experience placements.

In role, discuss whether work experience is an effective use of time for students in Year 11. Remember to make sure that everyone is able to contribute to the discussion and has a chance to give an opinion!

Activity 4

The headteacher has asked you to prepare an individual presentation to governors on the question:

Work experience: do we need it?

Remember, you must convince your audience to agree with your ideas, so be persuasive, but polite!

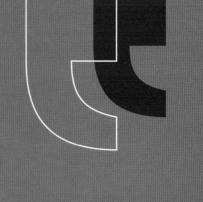

Reading

Learning objectives

In this unit you will be:

- retrieving and analysing information;
- improving your editing skills;
- developing your analysis skills – the technique question.

Text A: from The Mail Online, November 2014

Millions of youngsters are too sloppy and slovenly to get jobs because they lack the discipline or skills needed for work,' the Chief Inspector of Schools, Sir Michael Wilshaw, said yesterday. 'School and college leavers are careless about time, lack a work ethic, do not dress or speak well and are lackadaisical,' he added in his scathing remarks. 'Employers think teenagers and those in their early 20s have never been taught how to behave and work or about the attitude they need to get on.'

Sir Michael, head of Ofsted, said there was no point in keeping young people in education until 18 if they did not gain qualifications or were not prepared for the demands of work. 'If they dress inappropriately, speak inappropriately and have poor social skills, they are not going to get a job,' he continued.

Text B: Top 10 occupational areas for young people

Young people who left school in the 2009/10 academic year in the Falkirk area moved into a wide range of jobs. The bar chart below shows the top 10 occupational areas of local school leavers:

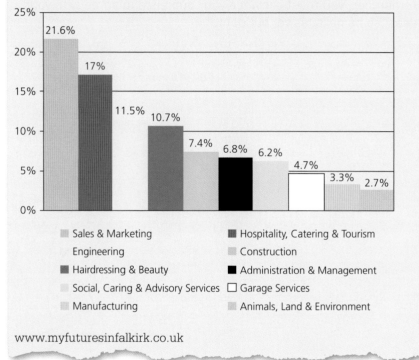

www.myfuturesinfalkirk.co.uk

Activity 5

1 The information in Text A refers to the word 'lackadaisical'. Select one definition from the list below that best defines this word:

   a unenthusiastic

   b troublesome

   c angry

   d helpless

2 Give five reasons, according to Sir Michael Wilshaw in Text A, why young people find it difficult to get a job.

3 What is the purpose of Text B? Is it:
  a personal
  b public
  c educational
  d occupational?
  Give two reasons for your selection.

4 Based on the evidence of the bar chart in Text B, how far do you agree with these statements?
  a More students tend to work in hotel industries than in caring and social work.
  b Careers in hairdressing and beauty are as popular as jobs in hospitality, catering and tourism.
  c More students decide to opt for sales work than manufacturing.
  d More students are interested in working with animals than working with cars.

Text C: Boardroom to classroom: why I swapped the FTSE 100 for teaching, by Katie Roberts (The Guardian, 26/5/2015)

I can't pinpoint the exact moment I decided to leave a corporate career spanning more than 20 years to teach children. I was successful and happy, yet I couldn't ignore the 'Is this it?' feeling that hit me each time I drove to work. I studied natural sciences at university and spent 14 years climbing the career ladder in a FTSE 100 business. But, eight years on, I couldn't shake the feeling that there must be something else to life.

Teaching came to mind as it combined my love of working with people alongside making a difference to children's lives. Changing career hasn't been easy but two years on I have no regrets. However, I had to put in some hard graft and get the basics right to break into teaching. I took a blow financially – selling the car and, much to my sports-mad family's dismay, cancelling our Sky subscription – but these are small prices to pay for such a rewarding career.

While friends were supportive, they thought I was mad to give up a career with great financial rewards. There were also negative reactions from teacher colleagues who were sceptical because I didn't have an educational background. My previous skills, however, helped me build relationships quickly and I found that most teachers unite around a common motivation: to make a difference to children's lives.

And you need that motivation. If you are thinking of entering teaching simply because of the long holidays, this won't be the ideal career change and you'll soon come unstuck.

You may get six weeks off in the summer, but it's likely that some of this will be spent planning for the new academic year and you'll have to put a lot of hard work into term time to pay for it. Expect to put in a few extra hours at the weekend and evenings, too, for marking and feedback.

One of the biggest challenges can be the physical demands of the job. You are on your feet and interacting with people almost all of the day, so you have to be someone who enjoys this.

If there were three pieces of advice I'd give someone thinking about a career change, they would be: research as much as you can from as many different angles, spend time with people who are already doing the job, and go through the positives and negatives so you're prepared, there are no surprises and you go in with eyes wide open.

For me, changing career was the right choice. The thing that makes me smile the most is when you see children believing in themselves. I have received some amazing, and humbling, feedback from the students. They make me feel that I'm making a difference every day, and nothing in the business world can compare to it.

(Katie Roberts is director of achievement for science at Heanor Gate Science College in Derbyshire)

Stretch

Think of a question that can only be answered by looking at two or more of the texts in this section. Write a response to this question.

Activity 6

1   Look at Text C on the previous page. What are the challenges that the writer has had to face in her career change? How did others react to the writer's decision to change careers?

Text D: from 'Nice Work' written by David Lodge (Vintage, 1988) about the experience of working in a foundry (a factory specialising in producing things made from metal moulds, such as wheels)

Even this warning did not prepare Jane for the shock of the foundry. They entered a large building with a high roof hidden in gloom. The place rang with the most barbaric noise Jane had ever experienced. The floor was covered with a black substance that looked like soot, but grated under her shoes like sand. The air reeked with a sulphurous smell and a fine drizzle of black dust fell on their heads from the roof. It was a place of extreme temperatures: one moment you were shivering in an icy draught from some gap in the wall, the next you felt the frightening heat of a furnace on your face. Everywhere there was indescribable mess and disorder. It was impossible to believe that anything new and clean and mechanically efficient could come out of this place.

Test yourself

Look at Text D. How does the writer make the working conditions seem unpleasant? Think about what the writer says and how he says it. [10]

Top tips

1   Write comments that link to the key word (unpleasant) in the question.
2   Underline the important words **within** the quotation to help you focus on 'the how'.
3   It can be a good idea to include the word 'by' in your answer as it is a signpost that you are beginning to look at the writer's techniques. For example,

The writer makes the foundry seem unpleasant by using dramatic language such as 'warning' and 'shock'. This suggests that Jane is completely unprepared and taken by surprise when she goes in to the foundry.

The table on the next page includes some evidence that you might use in your answer. In the first row, the word is underlined and explained. Can you complete this for the rest?

Evidence	How these are unpleasant
'high roof hidden in <u>gloom</u>'	Here the word 'gloom' suggests it is very dark and there is little light to relieve the workers' spirits.
'the place rang with the most barbaric noise'	
'the floor was covered with a black substance like soot'	
'the air reeked with a sulphurous smell'	
'a fine drizzle of black dust fell on their heads'	
'it was a place of extreme temperatures'	

Activity 7 Editing task

1 Circle the word below that best fits the gap in the sentence below:

Unemployment is a major .... of low self-esteem in young people.

   a reason
   b cause
   c friction
   d disappointment

2 Read the sentences below and then answer the questions that follow:

*He was sitting ....(1).......... outside the office. ....(2)..........
he would impress any potential employer with his qualifications
and enthusiasm?*

Circle the word below that best fits gap (1):
   a skilfully
   b confidently
   c suddenly
   d curiously

Circle the word that best fits gap (2):
   a However
   b When
   c Surely
   d Whereas

3 Read the text below which consists of sentences in the wrong order. Can you put these into the right order and try to explain how you decided on this order:

   1 I am a hard-working and ambitious student.
   2 I would like to take this opportunity to present you with my letter of application.
   3 This has been shown through my extensive qualifications and involvement in a range of extra-curricular clubs.
   4 Furthermore I have developed a strong ability to work well with others.

Stretch

Complete this paragraph with two further appropriate sentences.

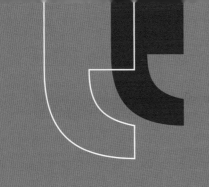

Writing

Learning objectives

In this unit you will be:

- adapting your style to suit form and purpose – newspaper report;
- developing proofreading skills;
- communicating ideas clearly in writing;
- developing narrative writing.

Activity 8 Put it to the proof

A reporter has brought this news report to check before it can be included in the newspaper. Identify and correct the errors. There are at least ten errors:

Anglers court up in voilent storm

Last night five people was rescued from a fishing boat that got into difficultys during a feirce storm off the coast of west wales. The ships captain had radioed the coast gard to report that the ship was in danger of sinking and that they were facing an emergancy situation.

'It was all rolling all over the place and I thoht it would sink he told our reporter.

What sort of errors did you spot? Identify these as Spelling, Punctuation or Grammar errors below.

Spelling	Punctuation	Grammar
e.g. feirce	e.g. no quote marks	e.g. expression errors

Activity 9

Read the extracts below from newspaper reports.

Text A: A Story of Swimming Success

Millie Jones is this morning celebrating her gold medal success in the Paralympics 200m breast stroke event.

Yesterday, in the packed Olympic pool in London, where the swimming event has been taking place all week, Millie swam the race of her life to finish in the gold medal position.

For any competitive athlete a gold medal is an incredible achievement, but for Millie it was also the result of years of determination, resilience and courage. The 25-year-old was just 10 when she lost her right leg as a result of a serious car crash. However, despite the pain and discomfort caused by her artificial leg, Millie never gave up and became even more determined to adopt a positive outlook and live life to the full.

When she joined the local swimming club she never dreamt that she would end up an Olympic champion.

Text B: Masked looters in daylight robbery

Yesterday, at approximately 14.20, a daring robbery occurred at Lloyds Bank in Stanley Road. Three men, wearing black balaclavas, stormed into the bank and are believed to have fled with over £1.5 million.

The thieves, carrying machetes and metal poles, entered the bank before violently threatening and attacking a security guard. They made their way to the cashier's window and demanded for a sports bag to be filled with money.

Abandoned

Witnesses revealed the men were wearing camouflaged trousers and black hoodies.

'They didn't raise their voice, just calmly demanded the money,' one customer told us.

It is believed that the thieves made their get-away in a black van which was later discovered abandoned on waste land.

Look at the following features and identify the ones you think relate to news reports – can you find an example of each one?

Features	Text A	Text B
short paragraphs		
use of third person (he/she)		
long paragraphs		
headlines		
direct speech		
past tense		
present tense		
emotive language		
first person (I)		
opening summary		
proper nouns		

Activity 10

The beginning of the well-known story of 'Goldilocks and the Three Bears' has been written below as a narrative story and as a news article/news report. Read the two versions below, and identify the similarities and differences (copy and complete the table below).

Narrative	Similarities	News report
Starts at the beginning.	Both use past tense.	Starts with a summary.

Version A

Goldilocks woke up one morning and decided she needed some excitement in her life. She swallowed a cup of tea and raced out of the house. Suddenly she saw a dark house in the distance and thought to herself, 'This looks interesting.' As she crept nearer she could see two round windows. When she looked into the first one, she was greeted by a pile of unwashed plates on the table.

Version B

Innocent girl nearly savaged by bears

Yesterday morning, a girl – later identified as Goldilocks – told us of her ordeal at the hands of a family of bears.

It had all started when she decided to go for a walk in the woods.

'The house looked really scary, but as it was raining I had to take cover. Little did I know that I would regret it,' she informed us.

Top tips

The way a character speaks can often suggest their personality. Instead of writing 'he said'/'she said', make sure your use of **verbs** is interesting and precise; e.g. 'he bellowed'/'she whispered'.

1 How many different words can you think of for the word 'said' that you often find in newspaper accounts?
2 Try to make a list of at least five alternatives, and decide what the words might suggest about the way the character is feeling.

Stretch

Choose another well-known fairy story and rewrite part of the story as a news report. You can use one these summaries as a starting point:

- Little Red Riding Hood: Wolf eats beloved grandmother and dresses up in her clothes in order to trap little girl.
- Sleeping Beauty: Princess falls into a hundred-year sleep and is finally woken by handsome prince.

Test yourself

Read the following exam-style question carefully.

> You have recently completed your work experience placement. There were some incidents that were especially funny, dramatic or memorable. Write a news report for a school newspaper which recounts a particular incident in the workplace. [35]

Planning your news report

The five-part plan is a commonly used structure for planning newspaper reports.

The answers to the first four questions (Who? What? When? Where?) should feature early on in your newspaper report. 'Why?' is often the basis of the rest of the article.

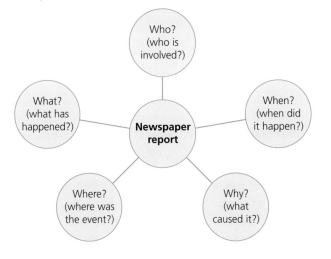

Spot four of the Ws in the opening sentence below:

> Yesterday afternoon, a group of king penguins escaped from London Zoo.

Top tips

As you will be narrating a sequence of events, consider the following:

1 Start with a **summary** of the facts that happened.
2 Organise your ideas **chronologically** (the order in which the events occurred).
3 Use a **headline** to give an idea of the event.
4 Create suitable **subheadings** to sum up each section of your report.
5 Use **time adverbs** to help move to the key events; e.g. 'A few hours later...', 'Next morning ...'.

Stretch

When you have finished writing your newspaper report, look back over your work and highlight examples of where you have used:

- **adjectives** and **adverbs** to engage the reader;
- **interesting** and **precise verbs**;
- **short paragraphs**;
- eye-catching **headline** and **subheadings**;
- **direct speech** to reveal feelings;
- **proper nouns** to show names and places.

How satisfied are you with what you have written?

- Write down two things you think you have done well.
- Write down two things you can improve on next time.

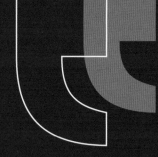

4c The perfect job

Oracy

Learning objectives

In this unit you will be:
- presenting information clearly;
- responding to ideas;
- interacting with others;
- drawing ideas together.

Activity 1

As a group you have been asked to consider what the 'perfect' job would be. Read the article below and then answer the questions that follow.

The coolest jobs in the world

Most people dream of escaping the rat race but that would not be the case if they had one of the best jobs in the world.

Penguinologist The Zoological Society of London have a resident penguinologist who specialises in anything and everything related to penguins. Among his various tasks Dr Tom Hart is researching the threats to Antarctic penguins. In 2011 he oversaw the largest penguin pool in the country at London Zoo.

Tastemaster Earlier this year Rich Keam from Brighton was selected as Western Australia's 'taste master' which will see him eat and drink his way around the state for six months and promoting it to the rest of the world. The job was advertised as part of a new campaign by the Australian tourist board which saw six candidates being hired for the 'best jobs in the world'.

Jester The tradition of court jesters may have come to an end when Charles I was overthrown but there are still plenty of professional fools. English Heritage has had its own jester since 2004 when 'Kester the Jester' was appointed. Kester was replaced by Peterkin the Fool who has also been Resident Fool at Hampton Court Palace since 1992.

Waterslide tester Earlier this year Sebastian Smith got the ultimate graduate job, as a waterslide tester for First Choice. The job involves riding and rating the company's water chutes in exotic locations. Smith's predecessor hung up his trunks after four years in the job which he called 'the best job in the world'. Smith will be expected to rate the slides for biggest 'splash' and 'adrenalin factor'.

Duvet tester Department store John Lewis employs a specialist duvet tester who picks out the most comfortable bedding for customers by testing it out first. Jo Unsworth is currently in the role and says, 'It's probably the only career where sleeping on the job is actively encouraged.'

Champagne taster The ultimate job in the champagne industry probably belongs to Olivier Krug who runs the House of Krug. It helps to be born into the business; he is sixth generation of his family to run the champagne house. Krug travels the world, supervises the grape harvest, and drinks lots of champagne. Once the champagne has been harvested Krug oversees the tasting committee which tries thousands of wines to check if they come up to scratch.

www.telegraph.co.uk, 22/10/2013

1 Write down a list of advantages and disadvantages connected with each job.

2 Which three of these six 'jobs' do you personally consider to be the 'coolest'? Make sure you can justify your choice!

3 In pairs or groups share your ideas and decide on the top three from the selection – or choose one of your own.

Activity 2

Study the list of 'The Worst Jobs of 2015'. In groups, what reasons can you suggest for these jobs being branded as 'worst'?

The worst jobs of 2015:

1 Newspaper reporter
2 Lumberjack
3 Enlisted military personnel
4 Cook
5 Broadcaster
6 Photojournalist
7 Prison officer
8 Taxi driver
9 Firefighter
10 Postman

Fortune.com/2015/04/15/worst-jobs/

Activity 3

In pairs, choose one of the chosen jobs and prepare seven questions that you would use to interview someone for the role. Remember that you need to find out if the person has the right qualities and attributes for the job.

Below are some questions that have been asked at interviews. Which questions do you think are most appropriate (and inappropriate)?

- What are your strengths/weaknesses?
- Why did you leave your last job?
- When and where were you happiest?
- Tell me about a time when things went badly.
- What experience do you have with ...?
- What would you do if you were the president of the world?

Top tips

When you conduct your interview, whether you are the interviewer or the interviewee, remember it will be a **formal situation**, and you may need to adapt and change your language to match this. You might find it useful to think about how some of the **informal** or **colloquial** expressions in the table could be changed to become more formal.

Activity 4

In pairs, conduct your mock interviews.

Informal/colloquial	Formal
I sorted it out ...	
Loads of ...	
Gonna ...	
It's up for grabs	
Wrap this up	
On the level	
Hang in there	

Stretch

Imagine your life in ten years' time. What type of job would you like to have? Would this be your 'ideal' job? What job do you think you will be doing?

Present your views on your ideal job to the rest of the class.

You might like to think about:
- the skills and qualifications needed;
- what interests you about this job;
- what the job actually involves;
- your hopes and ambitions for the future.

Reading

Activity 5

Text A is a leaflet to help new teenage weekend workers understand the rules at a company called All U Need. Read the extract and answer the questions that follow.

Text A: New workers must attend a health and safety training day on Saturday, November 27 2010

Health and Safety Rules

We ask you to:

- know where all the fire alarms are
- report to your manager anything which you think is dangerous, e.g. broken glass, wet floor, etc.
- report any accidents and make sure that they are written in the accident book
- only use equipment you have been trained to use
- follow the information given on all notices and warning signs
- know who the trained first-aider is when you are on duty.

Terms of Contract

1 Pay for:

   Ages 16–17   £4.00 per hour

   Ages 18–21   £4.95 per hour

2 Hours of work:

   Saturday 9.00 a.m.–6.00 p.m.

   Sunday 10.30 a.m.–4.30 p.m.

3 Holidays

   Your manager must be told two weeks before you plan to take time off.

4 Sickness

   You must phone as soon as possible to inform your manager if you are not fit to work.

5 Quitting your job

   You must give the manager two weeks' notice when you wish to stop working for All U Need.

(WJEC GCSE Functional Skills English exam paper)

1 What is the purpose of Text A? Is it:
   a personal
   b public
   c educational
   d occupational?

2 According to Text A:
   a What do you do if you are sick?
   b How much would you be paid if you were 18 years old?
   c What two things must be reported?
   d What two things should you find out in your first week at work?

Activity 6

Read through Text B, which is a newspaper report. In your own words, **summarise** the reactions of other people to Robbie's activities.

Text B: 'Suspended: 12-year-old boy who earns £200 a day selling chocolate to pals at his school'

A schoolboy has been suspended for selling chocolate and crisps to pupils. Robbie Twigg, 12, says he got the idea for his business from the TV show 'The Apprentice', and took inspiration from an episode which showed how to buy goods and then sell them on to make a profit.

His family says he was making up to £200 a day at his school. But the school has a strict healthy-eating policy and teachers say sales between pupils are banned.

Robbie first began selling the snacks bought from a retail park at the start of this term. He was sent home for a day and given a warning by teachers, but the budding businessman persisted in smuggling goods into the school – and has now had 10 days of suspensions, which most schools would use only for very serious behaviour issues.

His parents say they have tried to stop their son from selling the sweets – but believe his punishment is too harsh. His dad said: 'We are supporting the school and we've grounded him, and taken his phone off him as a punishment. We've told him not to do it and have checked his bag before he goes out, but he's only selling chocolate and the way they have dealt with it is far too harsh. The school has made it sound like he's selling cigarettes or something.'

'At the end of the day, the school sets the rules and that's fair enough. But I think he's just showing a bit of business sense and he shouldn't be missing out on his education because of it.'

The canteen at the school does not stock fizzy drinks or sweets, selling only healthy snacks and meals. Robbie buys his stock from bulk discount stores and wholesalers, selling to classmates at a higher price.

He said, 'The school just sells water and dinners. I've been bringing in eighty chocolate bars and stuff like fizzy drinks each day and have been selling out.'

He added, 'I've got a good business brain and when I watched "Dragon's Den" and then "The Apprentice" it gave me the idea of what to do. I saw stuff was going cheap, so I bought about £30 worth and I would sell it in the playground – some days I would make up to £200.'

The headteacher at Robbie's school said pupils were encouraged to develop their business skills through activities such as growing vegetables for sale but added, 'The private selling of goods on school premises is not permitted. Any activities which undermine our healthy-eating policy cannot be tolerated.'

However, other people have supported Robbie's enterprise. Commenting on the story, Charlie Mullins, a self-made millionaire who founded his own firm, said on an internet blog site, 'What better example could there be of a young businessman than Robbie? When he leaves school, I'll bet he'll be the person from his class making most money, and he'll also be creating jobs and employing his fellow pupils. The school needs some lessons in real life. The headteacher should have applauded Robbie's efforts instead of punishing him.'

(WJEC GCSE Foundation English Language paper, summer 2013)

Activity 7

Text C is an extract from a story about children on a work experience project. They are painting the house for an old lady called Mrs Malby. In the final line, we find out that Mrs Malby is 'unable to prevent her tears'. With reference to the text, explain what happens to make her cry.

Text C, extract from 'Broken Homes', by Ben Aaronovitch (Gollancz, 2013)

'Hi,' said the blond boy to her in the hall when she returned. He was standing combing his hair, looking at himself in the mirror. There were yellowish smears on the carpet, which upset Mrs Malby very much.

'Oh please, no!' she cried.

Yellow emulsion paint partly covered the pink of one wall in the kitchen. Some had spilt on to the vinyl floor and had been worked through.

'But I only said to wash them,' she cried.

One of the boys smiled at her, continuing to slap paint on the ceiling. A lot of it dripped back on top of him, on to the draining board and on to cups and saucers and cutlery and on the floor.

'Do you like this colour?' he asked.

Unsteadily, Mrs Malby crossed the kitchen and turned off the blaring radio.

'I said to wash the walls. I didn't even choose that colour. Please stop painting.'

'Are we in the wrong house? Only we was told …'

'You haven't come to the wrong house. Please wash off the paint and wipe it up where it's split on the floor.'

'No problem,' said the blond boy.

Not wishing to stay in the kitchen herself, she ran the hot tap in the bathroom and rubbed hard at the paint on the carpet in the hall. From the kitchen, above the noise of the radio, came the clatter of raised voices, laughter and a crash.

She sat for twenty minutes and then she went and knocked on the kitchen door. There was no reply. She pushed open the door gingerly.

More yellow paint had been splashed on. The whole wall around the window was covered with it, and most of the wall behind the sink. All four children were working with brushes. A tin of paint had been upset on the floor.

Mrs Malby stood there watching them, unable to prevent her tears.

Top tips

On the surface, this looks like a straightforward question that might be answered in a single line, e.g. the children mess up Mrs Malby's house.

However, the examiner will be looking at your ability to **track** the text and show some **inference** along the way, e.g.

The first thing Mrs Malby sees are the 'yellowish smears' on the carpet. This makes her 'upset', and the casual greeting, 'Hi', by the young boy suggests that he does not realise or care what he has done.

How has the example above used the text in their answer? Can you spot any inference or reading between the lines?

Text D is a newspaper article about how Jamie Oliver created a scheme to help trainee chefs find work.

Text D

When he was a young boy, Tim Siadatan, one of 14 children, had to work for four days a week after school to raise money to buy himself new clothes.

Today, after graduating as one of the final nine teenagers who survived Jamie Oliver's crash course in running a restaurant, Siadatan is planning to open his own chain of diners one day.

'Jamie has managed to completely change nine people's lives overnight,' he told *The Observer* in his first interview. 'What he has done is amazing; he's taught us that with passion and determination you can get any career you want and be a success; a real heavy-duty success.'

Siadatan, 19, was one of 15 young people picked by Oliver from 1,000 jobless hopefuls earlier this year to be filmed learning to cook in his new London restaurant, which he has called 'Fifteen'.

The resulting Channel 4 programme, *Jamie's Kitchen*, won record viewing figures as more than six million people turned in over five weeks to watch the often painful learning curve as the unemployed youngsters gradually transformed themselves into efficient semi-professionals. His book of the same name is now at the top of the bestseller list. The restaurant has become the most talked about venue in London, and Oliver eventually refused to take any more bookings after the restaurant became fully booked for five months ahead.

Now *Jamie's Kitchen* is finished, the real work is getting underway, with the young chefs working 18 hour days, six days a week, to satisfy the hordes of diners eager to test their new skills. 'Some of us joined this scheme as naïve, narrow kids,' said Siadatan. 'We have been transformed into incredibly focused, career-minded young people. Oliver has given us a passion for a career and has instilled a love for it in us. We love going to work and how many people can say that? We now all believe we can achieve something with our lives.'

(WJEC GCSE Foundation English Language paper)

Test yourself

Compare how the teenagers in Jamie Oliver's article are presented with the teenagers in Texts B and C.

Remember to state clearly the text you are taking your information from.

Copy and complete this table to scaffold your answer.

Text D	Text B	Text C
Independent: 'had to work … to buy himself new clothes'	Gets in trouble	Inept: 'smear'

[10]

Top tips

There are two parts to this question. First of all, look at how the teenagers are presented in Text D. When you compare this with the presentation of teenagers in Text B and Text C, focus on evidence from the other two texts **which focuses on teenagers only**.

Think about the connectives you could use to link your points. Some of these might be useful when writing your answer:

however   whereas   likewise   similarly   in contrast   in comparison   conversely   alternately

Sample student responses

Read through the student responses to this question.

- Which of these responses is the more successful?
- Why is this?
- What suggestions would you make to improve the other answer?

Student A

The writer tells us about how Robbie Twigg is quite intelligent and can make money even at the age he is. He took inspiration from an episode which showed him how to buy and sell things to make a profit. He had good tactics about selling things and all he is doing is getting them from a retail park and making a lot of money. This shows he has good business skills.

In contrast, the teenagers who paint Mrs Malby's house are shown to be careless, silly and disrespectful. Likewise in the text about Jamie Oliver, the teenagers are shown to be thoughtless and ungrateful. I think Robbie Twigg is the best example.

Student B

Firstly, we are told about how Robbie earns money at school through selling goods and making a profit. We are told that Robbie is inspired from episodes on TV such as *The Apprentice* which suggests he 'has a good business brain'. Evidence to support how good a business man Robbie is can be seen in the use of statistics; he makes £200 a day sometimes. We are told that when he was sent home, 'the budding businessman' persisted in doing so, resulting in a 10-day suspension. This tells us he has determination and a desire to succeed in business. Therefore, Robbie is presented as hard-working, resilient and determined.

Whereas in Text C the teenagers are shown to be reluctant to work and careless when they 'continue to slap paint on the wall' and 'smile to themselves'. In Text D the teenagers seem hard-working and grateful for the chance to change their lives as one says, 'We have been transformed into incredibly focused, career-minded young people.'

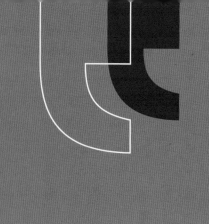

Writing

Activity 8 Put it to the proof

Your friend has applied for part-time work at a local hotel and has asked you to check the letter for mistakes before sending it. Find and correct any errors.

Dear Sir/madame

I am aplying for your advertisement on part-time staff. I have had experiance of this tipe of work and enjoy it. Im very well organised polt and good with people. I find that I am quick on my feet and react well in emergancies. I enjoy working as part of a team and cope well under presure.

What sort of errors did you spot? Identify these as Spelling, Punctuation or Grammar errors below.

Spelling	Punctuation	Grammar
e.g. aplying	e.g. no apostrophe	e.g. expression errors

Activity 9

Here are some different types of sentences.

1 Simple sentence. These sentences have a subject and one verb (an action word) and they give one piece of information. For example:

   The boy chased the ball.

2 Compound sentence. Two or more simple sentences are joined together by a **coordinating conjunction** like 'and', 'or', 'but'. These conjunctions can **only go in the middle of a sentence**:

   *The boy chased the ball **and** he scored a great goal. (correct)*

   ***And** the boy chased the ball he scored a great goals. (incorrect)*

3 Complex sentence. These sentences are called complex as they join two simple sentences by a **subordinating conjunction**. These are easy to spot as you can use these at the START of a sentence as well as in the middle:

   ***When** he left school he became a plumber. (correct)*

   *He became a plumber **when** he left school. (also correct!)*

There are many other different ways you can begin a sentence. For example, you could use a:

- pronoun (I, you, he, she, it, we, they)
- definite or indefinite article (the/a)
- preposition (on, in, against)
- -ing word (present participle)
- adverb (firstly, lastly, inevitably, of course).

Look at the following article written by a student giving his opinion about footballers' wages, and then answer the questions below.

> *I think it is unfair that footballers in this country earn so much money. It is unjust and scandalous. I think there should be a law that puts a limit on how much money they can earn. I think, for example, that top footballers shouldn't be allowed to earn more than one million pounds a year. I believe that a limit like this will make the game more fair and competitive and it might stop so many foreign players invading our league! I think it will help the teams in the lower leagues attract better footballers and as a result they will have a better chance of winning matches against the top teams. I also think that by doing this it will bring football back into the real world as many ordinary people feel that players are out of touch with their fans. I believe it is wrong that we seem to be valuing footballers more than doctors and nurses because they are paid so much money.*

1 What do you think the student could do to improve this piece of writing?

2 How can you vary the way each sentence is started here? Rewrite the paragraph.

3 When you have done this, pick out your favourite or the most effective sentence and explain your choice.

Top tips

When you are writing to explain your ideas, you will need to show that you can use different types of sentences.

Read through the definitions of different types of sentences. When you complete Activity 10, try to make use of **subordinating conjunctions** to vary your sentences, e.g.

  While   When   If   As   Although

Activity 10

When you are writing a guide it is important to try to gain a closer connection with the reader. How does the writer below create a 'rapport' (connection) with the reader in the advice given in the extract below about stopping smoking?

Think about use of:

- personal pronouns
- adverb starters/discourse markers
- abbreviations
- interesting punctuation
- varied sentences
- imperatives.

Using the features above, create a mind-map of examples from the text.

> *Out of every hundred of us who manage to puff our way through twenty cigarettes a day, over a quarter of us will die early because we have chosen to smoke cigarettes. Of course, we all have lots of reasons why we smoke: it's part of my scene; it's makes me feel cool; it keeps my weight down ... Blah, blah, blah ... Now look, we know it's bad for us. Not just bad. It's eventually truly awful. So, let's look at some ways we can cut down or stop smoking ...*

Top tips

Although this is an **exposition** task that may appear in Unit 2, you would expect the guide to give some valuable **advice** for students.

As your audience is Year 11 students, it is important to engage their interest and establish a connection with your audience.

Stretch

When you have finished, go back over your guide and highlight examples of the different language features you have used.

Test yourself

Choose one of these exam-style questions:

> Write a guide explaining how students can prepare themselves for their first job or college interview.

Or

> Write a guide explaining how students can survive their week of work experience. [35]

Plan your answer

Before starting (as with any extended writing task) it is important to PLAN your response. This need not take a long time (usually one or two minutes) but should help you write a more sustained response. Think of four or five areas that you want to cover. Each 'area' can be turned into a **heading** or **topic sentence starter**.

If the guide is about preparing for your first job interview, which of the following topics below are most appropriate headers or sections for this task?

Dress   Benefits   Preparation   First impressions   Ambitions

Travel   Hygiene   Relaxation   Questions

Unit 5: Citizenship

5a Charity

Oracy

> **Learning objectives**
>
> In this unit you will be:
> - interacting with others;
> - responding to questions and ideas;
> - drawing ideas together.

Activity 1

A local charity are considering opening a food bank in your town. You are not sure whether this is a good idea and decide to do some research. Read the texts below. Use Text A to identify reasons to set up a food bank, and Text B to note down any negative points.

Text A: Why do people use food banks?

Wandsworth food bank has fed more than 1,800 people since April 2014, up 30 per cent from last year. The food bank is just one of more than 400 operated by the Trussell Trust across the UK. Everyone who comes to the food bank is referred by a professional – such as a social worker, teacher or local GP.

Sarah Chapman, who set up the Wandsworth food bank in 2013, told Channel 4 News: 'The food part of a budget is always the part that will be squeezed.

One family were referred to us by the children's school. Their dad had been stopped in a shop the weekend before for shoplifting potatoes and a tin of beans – he was desperate.'

The biggest reason for referral to Wandsworth food bank was benefit delays and benefit changes, accounting for 44 per cent of users. Twenty-three per cent of referrals were because of low income.

Trussell Trust guidelines say that households should be given three days' worth of food per crisis, but often food banks have little choice but to support families for longer. A crisis can be anything from losing a job to domestic violence to benefit delays.

Chris Mould, chairman of the Trussell Trust told Channel 4 News: 'We provide every year. We know that if they don't get help from us or another provider they would be forced to look elsewhere. That might be that they commit a crime, shoplift or might lose their homes because they find it too difficult to pay the rent.'

www.channel4.com

Text B: No ID, no checks … and vouchers for sob stories: The truth behind those shock food bank claims

One of the UK's biggest food banks last night pledged to investigate after volunteers were filmed admitting that people could take free food without checks.

One worker said that people regularly 'bounce around' locations to receive more vouchers than they are entitled to. A Mail on Sunday investigation has also found inadequate checks on who claims the vouchers, after a reporter obtained three days' worth of food simply by telling staff at a Citizen's Advice Bureau – without any proof – that he was unemployed.

Undercover reporters also found:

- Staff at one centre gave food parcels to a woman who had visited nine times in just four months, despite the rules that individuals should claim no more than three parcels a year.

- Staff at a supermarket, where shoppers are encouraged to buy extra food and donate it to a local food bank, were alleged to be later turning up to claim the food themselves.

Another volunteer revealed: 'Some people just grab at everything and even complain that the product is a cheap one and not the brand they want.'

Senior MP, Brian Binley, said, 'There are a lot of dishonest people who will cadge their way into situations. Food banks are run by very kind people. They do not understand that there are some people who will take advantage.'

www.dailymail.co.uk

Stretch

How is Text A written differently from Text B? Compare form, purpose and audience as a starting point, then look at language and structure.

Activity 2

Consider two advantages and two disadvantages of setting up a food bank. In pairs or groups, spend five minutes putting your case for or against a new food bank in your area.

Activity 3

You decide to attend a meeting about whether a food bank should be set up in your town. In groups of four, take on one of the roles below.

Your role is: **Charity member in favour of the food bank**. You consider that the town desperately needs a food bank. You wish to discuss: - the problems some people face without access to a food bank - ideas for collecting donations, raising money and organising the running of the food bank - how the idea of a food bank can be 'sold' to the people of the town.	Your role is: **Council representative against the food bank**. You are worried that the food bank will end up costing the council money. Your concerns are: - Where will the food bank be, and who will run it? - Might the fact that a food bank is needed in the town reflect badly on the council?
Your role is: **Local resident in favour of the food bank**. You intend to put forward: - the benefits of food banks - ideas for organising donations, storing and managing the distribution of food - counterarguments to any disadvantages that are suggested.	Your role is: **Working parent against the food bank**. Living next to a community centre, you are worried that the food bank will be set up right by your house. Your concerns are that: - the flow of food bank visitors will be disruptive - there will be abuses of the food bank and arguments. You suggest how those struggling to buy food could be **helped** instead of appealing to food banks.

1 Spend five minutes jotting down more ideas for or against the food bank.

2 Hold your meeting to discuss whether the food bank should be set up. Remember to stay in the role you have been assigned, and discuss a range of opinions that your character is likely to hold.

3 Decide whether the setting up of a food bank should go ahead. A chairperson should report the final decision and explain the reasons for coming to this decision.

Stretch

Take on the role of chairperson, and open the discussion.
- Encourage every speaker to offer ideas.
- Keep everyone focused on the task.
- Ensure that the discussion is not controlled by one or two speakers.
- Summarise ideas and key points.
- Encourage a conclusion.

Activity 4 Summing up

When you have completed the group discussion, present your decision to the class with reasons for your choice.

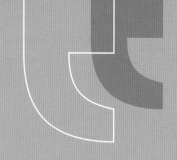

Reading

Learning objectives

In this unit you will be:
- retrieving information;
- editing texts;
- analysing non-fiction texts.

Activity 5 Editorial skills

Read the extract below, taken from the text in the opening section. Discuss how you could make it more emotive, using some of the features of language you identified.

Why do people use food banks?

Wandsworth food bank has fed more than 1,800 people since April 2014, up 30 per cent from last year. The food bank is just one of more than 400 operated by the Trussell Trust across the UK. Everyone who comes to the food bank is referred by a professional – such as a social worker, teacher or local GP.

Stretch

Extend your new version of the text so that it could be used as a charity appeal.

Activity 6

Read the following extract.

Amnesty International is the world's largest human rights _____(1)_____ of over 7 million people. It works to _____(2)_____ people whose human rights are _____(3)_____ by war and oppressive governments. Amnesty wants to help the most _____(4)_____.

Choose the word which best fits the gap:

1	organisation	club	meeting	membership
2	secure	lead	protect	preserve
3	anticipated	frightened	threatened	intimidated
4	judged	hated	biased	disadvantaged

Activity 7

Read the text below which consists of sentences in the wrong order. Show your understanding of the text by **sequencing** the sentences into a logical order, and give reasons for your choices.

1 This is due to insufficient charity funds, which often means that refugees have to stay in the camps for years.

2 These include children and the elderly.

3 When refugees first arrive at these camps, the most vulnerable are identified.

4 Refugee camps are usually built and run by international charities.

5 Despite the vulnerability of these groups, there are few provisions at the camp.

Activity 8

An **emotive** text aims to appeal to the reader's feelings. In a promotion or advertisement, the vocabulary used will simply try to sell the product. However, a charity leaflet may use language to gain the reader's sympathy.

Read this text that deals with the **emotive** issue of refugees. Identify as many examples of emotive language as you can, and comment on the effect that these have on the reader.

> **Torrential rains and thick mud are latest hurdles for refugees**
>
> As if fear, hunger, thirst, worry and exhaustion were not enough, new trials emerged yesterday for those on the 1,000-mile-plus trek into Europe: torrential rains and thick mud.
>
> About 7,000 refugees, including families with young children, braved relentless downpours to cross Greece's northern border into Macedonia.
>
> At the northern village of Idomeni, crowds gathered before dawn, using anything they could find – plastic sheeting, garbage bags, hooded jackets, even a beach umbrella – in a futile attempt to stay dry. Sneakers stuck in the mud. Rain dripped off hoods and caps. All were soaked to the skin.
>
> (From *The Independent* online, 11/09/2015: www.independent.ie)

To look more specifically at what effect these words have, you can start to look at the range of techniques that the writer has used.

Term	Evidence from text	Effect on reader
Emotive adjective		
Abstract noun		
Listing		
Statistics		
Powerful verbs		

Activity 9

Read this article and answer the question that follows.

Text A

What's happening?

Refugee children are frightened, homeless and many have witnessed unspeakable horrors. You can help them.

Europe is facing its worst refugee crisis since the Second World War.

So far this year, more than 350,000 desperate people have made the perilous journey across the Mediterranean Sea.

In Italy, 7,600 children have arrived alone since January, without any parents or families at all. For those who do survive the treacherous journey, the terrifying ordeal is not over. Children often arrive in Europe scared and exhausted.

Many have seen and experienced untold horrors during their journey.

The physical impact of travelling is also clear. The children our teams have met have had severe sunburn and blisters from their journey. Many have lost their toenails from the huge distances they had walked.

What we're doing

We work along the whole route that refugees take, as well as in the countries they are fleeing. In countries like Turkey, Greece and Italy, we provide children and their families with essentials that they desperately need – like food, water and shelter, as well as items like soap and toilet paper. We also run centres where children can shower, receive medical help and make calls.

We also continue to work in countries like Syria, where brutal war has ripped apart the lives of millions, as well as neighbouring countries where many have fled to, such as Lebanon and Jordan. Here, we provide children and their families with much needed food, safe water, medicine and shelter.

We also help children to return to school, make sure that they are getting the psychological support they need, and run literacy and numeracy centres.

How you can help

We're doing whatever it takes to provide essential support to the thousands of children in need but we desperately need your support to respond to this crisis.

PLEASE DONATE TO OUR CHILD REFUGEE CRISIS APPEAL

Your donation will support our work with refugee children.

Contact Us

If you have any questions about making a donation to Save the Children, please call+44 (0)20 7012 6400.

With your help, we can help even more children wake up to a bright future. Sign up to receive news from Save the Children or find out how to get involved here: www.savethechildren.org.uk/get-involved

www.savethechildren.org.uk

What evidence does the text use to support the statement that 'Europe is facing its worst refugee crisis'?

Test yourself

How does the writer persuade us to donate to the charity? You must support your comments by looking at the language and techniques the writer has used. In your response you should:

- refer to a **range** of evidence from the text;
- include **explanations** that **link** to the focus of the question;
- try to comment on **technique** as well as **content** for higher band marks. [10]

Look at the table below and identify where the student has been most successful in explaining their ideas. How would you improve the less successful explanations?

Evidence	How it persuades us to donate
'witnessed unspeakable horrors'	This helps to persuade us by using very emotive adjectives to make us feel pity for the refugees.
'worst refugee crisis'	The writer uses a superlative for effect.
'350,000 desperate people'	The writer uses statistics to appeal to us.
'the terrifying ordeal is not over'	The writer suggests that the experience has been awful and that there may be worse things to come.

Writing

Activity 10 Put it to the proof

You have been sent an email that appears to be from someone asking for help from you. Find the mistakes in the text that show you that this is not a genuine request for help but a fake appeal designed to trick you into sending money to a stranger.

Untitled - Message (HTML)

File   Message   Insert   Options   Format Text   Review   Adobe PDF

To...

Cc...

Subject:

Dear friend,

I know that you will be wishing to help me as I have leanred alot about your kindness from good freind of yours who past your email address to me I am now relying on you as I do not now what to do.

I am on holiday in Casablanca. Last night, during walking back to my hotel through Park, someone snached my bag. This bag contained my Pass Port and walet. I have gone to the police but they not help as I do not have any identificaton on me. They say that I must buy a passport release form so that I can travel to UK.

This form is only until tommorow morning and the last plane tonight leaves just before midnight. This is only chance. I am so upset because the police will not except that I do not have money. I really need you to send me €1000 in the link below or cannot come home. Please help me and I will give the money to your friend as soon as I am arriving back in the UK.

Thank you for your kindness good friend.

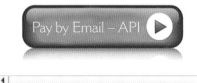

Pay by Email – API

What sort of errors did you spot? Identify these as Spelling, Punctuation or Grammar errors below. There are nine spelling, four punctuation and nine grammar errors to find.

Spelling	Punctuation	Grammar
e.g. leanred	e.g. no full stop	e.g. expression errors

Activity 11

Read the following extracts taken from different speeches. Identify:
- the form, purpose and likely audience of each – the 'context';
- how the language is suited to this context.

Text A

Thank you all for being with us and supporting this important event. Tonight is about raising as much as we can to help those families affected by the recent disaster. As a community, we want to give something to support those who have suffered so keenly over the past few challenging weeks.

Text B

Good evening. Here are tonight's headlines. The volcanic eruption at Mount Unzen, Japan, has now claimed over a hundred lives. Rescue workers are at the scene, sifting through rubble, in the hope of finding survivors.

Text C

I am delighted to have this opportunity to tell you a little about the Gothalo Centre in Kathmandu and explain why it is a place so close to my heart. My trip there was an incredible experience and I look forward to sharing it with you tonight.

My journey began a few months ago, when I happened to read an article in the paper about the children who had been orphaned by the Nepal earthquake.

	Form	Purpose	Audience	Language
Extract A	Welcome speech at a charity event			Polite opener used
Extract B				
Extract C				

Activity 12

Read the following extracts taken from persuasive speeches. Complete the table with examples of the techniques you find in each text. **Note that this is not a checklist, and not every technique will appear in every text.**

Some are completed for you.

Text A

It is a sad fact that the children's home receives no government funding, subsidies or grants at all. 100% of our revenue comes from donations and money raised at charitable events. Our accountants say that the centre faces closure within two years if we cannot raise more much needed cash. Now, it may seem that we are fighting a losing battle, but I am confident that you can help! It is through the kind contributions of people like yourselves, that our vital work can continue.

Text B

A quarter of children in Lesotho will never be given the opportunity to go to school. If they do, the resources are so limited, that they may find themselves sharing one reading book between ten pupils. However, the charity, Unicef, says that this can change. With reading books, text books and stationery sent from schools in the UK, we can make a real difference.

Text C

I ask you today – have you ever feared for your life when walking to school? Have you stayed inside because going out is too dangerous? Have you waved your father off to work and wondered if he would return? Tragically, this is the reality for children in war torn countries. You may feel that you can do nothing to change this. Think again.

Techniques	Text A	Text B	Text C
Strong, emotive language	'losing battle,' 'vital'		
Facts/statistics			
Expert opinion			
Tripling			
Personal pronouns			
Dramatic punctuation and rhetorical questions			

Test yourself

You would like students in your school to donate money to a charity that you care about. Choose a charity, real or imagined, and write a speech to be presented in school assembly. Your speech should aim to persuade students to donate money to the cause.

Include:

- who the charity helps;
- how it helps;
- examples/case studies of past help that it has provided;
- details of how students' donations will benefit;
- how students can donate money. [20]

Stretch

Use the table in Activity 12 to identify the techniques you have used in your own speech.

Sample student response

I ask you today, do you care about rabbits? Did you know that over 200,000 rabbits worldwide every year are used in horrifying experiments? They have chemicals rubbed in their fur, shampoo squeezed in their eyes and are forced to breathe in poisonous fumes.

Most of these experiments are not necessary. They are done to test whether shampoo's and body lotion's are suitable for humans but there is no need for these products to be put on animals. Computer programmes can assess whether humans are likely to react to products and paid human volunteers can also test the products themselves. However, it is cheaper and easier for big companies to use animals.

The rabbits are kept in cold, cramped cages in the laboratries. They wait in terror for the next dreadful expereiment to be performed. When it is time, they are taken from their cages and held down on testing benches. These animals cannot speak but that doesn't mean that they don't feel pain.

As these expereiments happen behind closed doors, most people don't think about them but that doesn't mean that they're not going on. Charities campagne against this cruelty and you can help by giving a small amount to animal charities to help them in their fight against animal testing.

Do you know what happens after a rabbit has been tested on? You might think that the animals might be taken to a centre to be cared for. Unfortunately this is not what happens. Even if the drugs and chemicals tested on the rabbit have irritated it, the product can still be sold to humans because human skin does not react the same as animal skin. This makes the expereiment worthless. Also, every rabbit that is tested on is either caged again to have another expereiment on it or is brutally killed.

It is because of this dreadful and horrifying experimentation that we all have a duty to help. By donating to anti-testing animal charities you can make a real difference and force our voices to be heard. *(340 words)*

Examiner comment:

Communicating and organising

This is an apt but slightly awkward opening. The student has held the reader's interest with some persuasive techniques. The writing is developed with some imagination and an appropriate tone. The speech is purposeful and relevant and the final paragraph is well-judged.

Writing accurately

The work is clearly organised and paragraphed. Apostrophes are sometimes used to form plurals and there are a few words spelled incorrectly (*laboratries, expereiment, campagne*). The student uses a variety of simple, complex and compound sentences accurately.

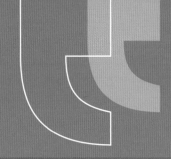

5b Clubs, societies and volunteering

Oracy

Learning objectives

In this unit you will be:

- responding to ideas;
- interacting with others;
- drawing ideas together;
- presenting information clearly.

Activity 1

Read the following summaries of possible activities for young people in your area.

Text A: 'The Rambers' (local walking group)

The group meets weekly, on Sunday afternoons. They choose a different route every week and the group consists of all ages from 7–70. They focus on aspects of history and geographical features of the local area and sometimes help with environmental projects.

Text B: 'Upstaged' (young people's theatre group)

The group consists of people aged 11–25 and they rehearse twice weekly (more when a show is imminent). They stage two shows a year, and these are a mix of comedies, serious dramas and musicals.

Text D: 'Sports 4 U' (youth club sports team)

Your local youth club has a number of sports teams that young people can join. They refine the skills of their members in their chosen sport and offer the opportunities to play in competition. Members can also help out with junior teams and organise and encourage children to take up the sport.

Text C: Army cadets

There are over a thousand cadet detachments in the UK. Although not officially part of the British Army, you will get a free uniform and opportunities to participate in thrilling activities like abseiling, rock climbing and mountain biking. Activities are provided at very low cost, or are often even free. Recruits can work towards recognised qualifications.

Text E: 'Click' (computer club)

The local computer club is looking for members. There are several aims – the club is a chance for people to game against others in competition, swap games and exchange tips. They also run a 'Silver Surfers' section, where young people help older people to learn how to use computers, tablets and smart phones. They also offer their members opportunities to develop skills in coding, website design and a range of applications.

Text F: 'Harmony' (young people's choir)

The choir attracts nearly 100 young people from all over the area. They specialise in singing contemporary songs and perform in venues all over the country. The choir runs an overseas trip every year. They have a competitive choirmaster who enters a number of competitions and is hoping that 'Harmony' will take part in a TV talent show next year. They are also planning to release a CD.

Activity 2

In **pairs**, discuss the following:
- The possible pros and cons of each activity.
- What further information would you like to have about each activity?
- What skills does each activity help to develop?
- Which three activities appeal to you most, and why?

Stretch

Add to the description of your top three activities by developing details of your own, and adding the skills that would be developed.

Activity 3

You have been asked to speak to a new Year 7 assembly about activities they can get involved with in the local area.

In the assembly, you will only have time to talk about three possibilities from the six options on the list.

Consider which three options you would promote.

Think about:
- what would be the benefits of getting involved in each activity;
- having as much variety across the year group as possible;
- what you think would appeal to this age group.

Discuss your choices. Can you come to some agreement on the three most appropriate activities to promote? Remember to consider your **target audience** (Year 7 students) in the content, tone and style of your delivery.

Stretch

You have been asked to put forward an idea of your own to replace one of the group's options. Research this extra option and consider what you will say about it.

Activity 4

Present your assembly. Consider how your choices can be 'sold' to your year group as exciting opportunities for getting involved in your local community, and the advantages for yourself and others.

Reading

Activity 5 Editing skills

Read the following first-hand accounts from participants in the Duke of Edinburgh awards, and answer the questions that follow.

'It's hard to remember my first _____(1)_____ but the expedition side of things really caught my eye and, even though this can be the most _____(2)_____ part of the Award, it was a form of escape and gave me the opportunity to get out in the hills with a team to complete an _____(3)_____.'

1 Select the words that best fit the gaps.

   1 institution   impression   individual   inconsequence

   2 brave   wonderful   exciting   challenging

   3 objective   dream   opportunity   ordeal

'The Award was offered to young people as a way to get involved in positive, _____(1)_____ activities. It provided kids with an opportunity to get out of the neighbourhood. Everyone is going to take something different from the Award but I think it remains extremely _____(2)_____ for young people today. There is still a need for young people to grow and build character; I think there is always a place for the Award, _____(3)_____ of your background and where you start from.'

2 Select the words that best fit the gaps.

   1 pointless   plentiful   meaningful   numerous

   2 inspirational   fun   repugnant   relevant

   3 whatever   regardless   reference   relevant

Activity 6

Read the extracts below and then answer the questions that follow.

Text A: An online news article about volunteering

The volunteers who help make Welsh attractions great

Those who work for free are the lifeblood of Welsh museums, galleries and stately homes.

Volunteers are the glue that holds many local and regional museums and charitable organisations together, but it can be easy to look past them when we visit. What motivates someone to give their free time to help ensure these attractions give us as visitors the most they can?

Sophia Kier-Byfield, 22, is a volunteer at Clore Discovery Centre and an Archaeology Archive volunteer for the Photography Archival Project based at the National Museum Cardiff.

'Volunteering in museums has been a central aspect of my life for the past two years. Not only is it a way to gain vital work experience and explore potential career pathways, it is also an enjoyable and rewarding opportunity to make museums more accessible and exciting for others.

'By helping to run workshops for children of all ages and abilities in the Clore Discovery Centre, I have had the chance to be creative and encourage children to become interested in museums and all of the fascinating historical, scientific and artistic artefacts and objects that can be found there.

'Also, by working alongside professionals from the museum on a project in conjunction with the Archaeological Department, I have learnt new skills, such as how to clean and archive photographs, which will hopefully help my academic career development in the future.

'Volunteering at the museum has been an exceptionally valuable and worthwhile venture. Indeed, museums all over the country are dealing with financial cuts, so in order to prevent the loss of collections and events that keep people of all ages interested and engaged, I would encourage others, where possible, to give some time to their local museum.'

www.walesonline.co.uk

Text B

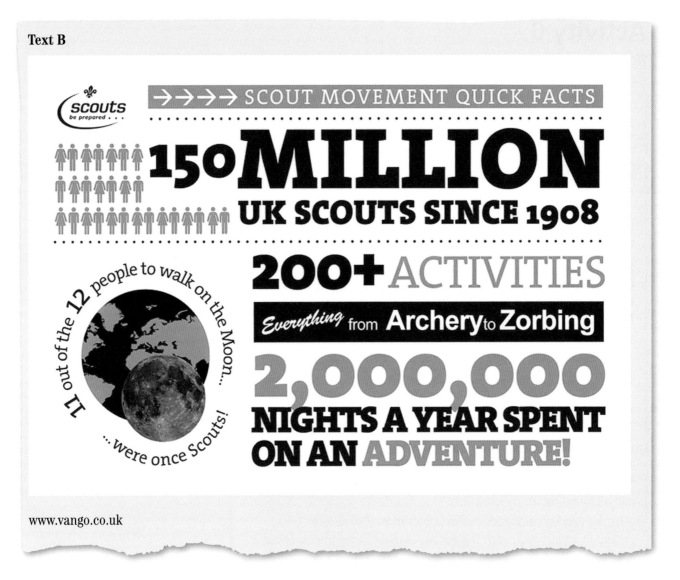

www.vango.co.uk

1 Look at Text A. Only one of the following is a fact. Which one is it?
   a Those who work for free are the lifeblood of Welsh museums, galleries and stately homes.
   b Volunteering at the museum has been an exceptionally valuable and worthwhile venture.
   c It is also an enjoyable and rewarding opportunity.
   d I have learnt new skills, such as how to clean and archive photographs.

2 'Those who work for free are the lifeblood of Welsh museums, galleries and stately homes.'
   a What does the word 'lifeblood' mean in this context?
   b Find one more metaphor in the next paragraph. What does this metaphor suggest about volunteers?

3 Look at Text B. Explain two ways in which the text states that there are a wide range of activities carried out by Scouts.

4 What does the fact about astronauts imply about joining the Scouts?

Text C: Get involved

We are always looking for people to join us and would love to welcome you along to Neath Little Theatre. Being a member of the theatre is a rewarding and enjoyable hobby and a great way to meet new people.

Acting, Directing, Set Building, Lighting, Sound, Props, Wardrobe, Stewarding, Hospitality, Tickets or Maintenance – there truly is a job for everyone, regardless of your background, age or experience. All we need from you is commitment and a desire to get stuck in!

If you would like to get involved, the best thing to do is come along to one of our Thursday Club Nights. You can simply turn up between 7 and 7.30p.m. (admission £2 for non-members). We understand that this can be quite daunting, so why not let us know via Facebook or email that you are coming and we will arrange for one of our members to meet you on arrival, show you around and introduce you to others.

www.neathlittletheatre.co.uk

TEXT D: extract from *Love Over Scotland* by Alexander McCall Smith (Abacus, 2006)

Bertie is a young boy who lives with Irene his mother. In this extract, Irene is forcing Bertie to join an orchestra.

'Hurry up now, Bertie,' said Irene. 'It's almost ten o'clock, and if we don't get there in time you may not get your audition. Now, you wouldn't want that, would you?'

Bertie sighed. To miss the audition was exactly what he would want, but he realised that it was fruitless to protest. Once his mother had seen a notice about the Edinburgh Teenage Orchestra, she had immediately put his name down for an audition.

'Do you realise how exciting this is?' she said to Bertie. 'This orchestra is planning to do a concert in Paris in a couple of weeks. Wouldn't you just love that?'

Bertie frowned. The name of the orchestra suggested that it was for teenagers and he was barely six. 'Couldn't I just audition in seven years' time?' he asked his mother. 'I'll be a teenager then.'

'If you're worried about being the youngest one there,' said Irene reassuringly, 'then you shouldn't! The fact that it's called the Edinburgh Teenage Orchestra is neither here nor there. The word teenage is just to indicate what standard is required.'

'But I'm not a teenager,' protested Bertie helplessly. 'They'll all be teenagers. I promise you. I'll be the only one in dungarees.'

'There may well be others in dungarees,' said Irene. 'And anyway, once you're sitting down behind your music stand, nobody will notice what you're wearing.'

Bertie was silent. It was no use; he would be forced to go, just as she had forced him to go to yoga and to all the rest of it. There was no use protesting. If he was unable to persuade his mother not to subject him to the humiliation of being the youngest member, by far, of an orchestra, then he would have to find some other means to ensure he did not get in.

Top tips

This is partly a mix of **what** is said and **how** it is said. See below for sample student responses to question 1.

Activity 7

1 How does the writer of Text C on the previous page try to persuade the reader to join Neath Little Theatre?

Sample student responses

In answering question 1 above, which one of these sample responses focuses on what is said, and which on how it is said?

Student A

The text persuades by saying what there is to do at the theatre. It mentions a whole range of things to do that includes 'acting, directing and set building' so there is something for everyone.

Student B

The text persuades by listing a wide variety of areas the reader can get involved with at the theatre. 'Acting, Directing, Set Building, Lighting, Sound, Props, Wardrobe ...' The list is long and makes it seem as if there is plenty of choice so may persuade the reader to get involved.

The text also offers opinions, such as being a member is 'rewarding and enjoyable'. These are presented as fact in order to convince. The writer uses the pronoun 'we' which gives a sense of togetherness and belonging, making you more likely to turn up.

Top tips

Track through the text carefully and select information that tells you something about what Bertie is thinking and feeling. Think about using a 'quote – explain' model (example in the table).

2 Look at Text D on the previous page. What are Bertie's thoughts and feelings in these lines? Create a table like the example below.

Evidence	Thoughts and feelings
'Bertie sighed.'	Bertie seems fed up.
'He realised that it was fruitless to protest.'	He knows it is pointless to speak up against his mother.

Writing

Activity 8

Which of following statements best describes argumentation writing?

Argumentation writing is a form of writing that …

a … is used in drama to explain what the actors do.

b … gives the reader the author's views and reasons for this viewpoint.

c … instructs the reader on how to do something.

d … describes a person, place or thing.

Activity 9

A teacher guide states:

Argumentation is a form of writing which presents a view of a topic. Students may find themselves considering a range of viewpoints on a given topic.

A topic is an issue for which there are arguments on both sides of the debate, for example, whether school uniform should be compulsory in schools, or whether contact sports for young people are a good thing.

Think of a range of topics that could be used for argumentation writing.

Activity 10

When approaching this form of writing, try to consider points for and against a topic. You may be giving your view from one side, but it is important to think of the opposing viewpoints in order to give a response to them. When you have considered both sides, summarise your view on the topic.

Consider the idea of having **compulsory residential outdoor pursuits days for all school children**. Think of **three** separate points to argue for and against this.

Use the table on the next page as a model for your thinking.

For	Against
My view:	

Activity 11

Read the following example of a review which puts forward a viewpoint:

> *'Man Of Steel' takes itself seriously. But it arguably needs to as it is returning to the cinema that is filled with other super-heroes like Thor, Iron Man, Hulk and the Avengers. While 'Man Of Steel' has a few irritating lapses (while the source of our hero's power is explained, it's unclear where Zod and his cronies get their abilities from), you can appreciate the way Goyer has filmed this. There is dramatic tension throughout: not only is he an illegal immigrant, he's a man-sized weapon of mass destruction. Of course the US government will distrust him. While 'Man Of Steel' won't outdo 'Avengers' in its snappy dialogue and humour, it certainly tops it when it comes to spectacle.*

> *'Man Of Steel' is* huge. *It opens on Krypton, a world of volcanoes and huge, bellowing, reptile monsters. It's a ravaged world which recalls 'The Matrix's horrifying landscape. Giant spacecraft soar through its burnt skies, as do strange, flying creatures. When a movie features Russell Crowe riding a dragon during its opening act, you have to take notice.*

Find at least one example and consider the effect of the following features used by the writer in the review:

Writing feature	Example	Effect
Bold statements		
Evaluative adjectives		
Adverbs like 'of course', 'arguably'		
Modal verbs, e.g. should, have to		
Connectives which evaluate, e.g. 'while'		
An occasional switch to second person		

Activity 12

The Headteacher has asked you to review the success (or otherwise) of one (or more) of the trips or activities that have taken place in schools. In your review you need to acknowledge other viewpoints on these trips, but be clear on your own thoughts and feelings about this topic.

The following words and phrases may help you to formulate ideas. Think about how they might be relevant to the trip and whether they might link to a positive or negative view of the trip.

money   teamwork   fitness   job prospects

experiences family   trust   responsibility

routine   society   enjoyment   comfort zone

You may also want to conduct some research to find relevant data, facts and opinions which you think may be helpful to you.

Complete a table like the one in the previous activity to help you plan for this task.

Activity 13

Read the opening paragraph below of an answer to the task.

EuroDisney is one of those places that everyone should visit. It was, therefore, more of a public service that the school offered in giving all pupils in the school a chance to visit. It is an amazing place, full of the characters everyone loves no matter how old they are. The rides are great, even if you have to queue a long time and the food is slightly over priced but tasty. Some people might argue that the trip is not educational. Well, I disagree. I learned a lot by going and I'm sure lots of people were the same. I for one, can't wait to go back! Très bien!

What advice would you give the student in terms of:

1 structure
2 adding detail and expanding on points
3 paragraphing
4 sentence structure?

Test yourself

Read the following exam-style question carefully:

Write a review of your experience of one of the following:

1 volunteering or fund-raising
2 a local group or society
3 a school trip. [20]

Ensure you use a range of techniques suited to task and audience. Which of the following could be useful in this task?

rhetorical questions	upbeat tone	subheadings
exclamations	second person	statistics
formal register	puns	first person
personal anecdotes	informal register	third person
connectives	evaluative adjectives	adverbs

Stretch

Can you think of any other techniques that might be useful?

Top tips

In the opening section:
1 Separate your review into sections, each addressing a benefit that joining a club or volunteering may have; for example, 'Meeting new people'. You will need to plan these areas in advance. Devote a section of your guide to each of these areas.
2 Organise the sections logically – you may want to number the ideas on your plan to get them in the best order.
3 Summarise the benefits of joining or volunteering in the final section.

5c Are teenagers given a bad press?

Oracy

Learning objectives

In this unit you will be:
- presenting information clearly;
- responding to ideas;
- interacting with others;
- drawing ideas together.

Activity 1

A resident has written a letter to your headteacher complaining about the behaviour of teenagers in the local area. Here is an extract from the letter:

> *'They ruin our environment, they ruin our streets and they ruin our peace and quiet. Badly behaved teenagers are out of control and they ruin everything for the rest of us. We need to control tearaway teenagers before it's too late.'*

Think about three negative and three positive impressions that people have about teenagers in your local community.

Activity 2

Read the following texts and discuss the way teenagers are presented in each text:

Text A is a magazine article written by a young person who has had problems with alcohol:

When I look back at my life between the ages of 15 and 18 I realise how utterly stupid I was to let alcohol control my life. It had started with me having a few drinks with my mates when we went to parties. We had watched adverts on the TV, and drinking alcohol looked fun. Some of us used to buy a few cans of cider or a bottle of vodka and go down to the park and drink them. Even though I did not have a job, I had plenty of money and was surprised that it was not too expensive to buy alcohol. There were one or two shops near where I lived which did not seem to bother about our age, so it was easy to buy alcohol.

(WJEC Functional Skills English exam paper)

Text B is a magazine article:

Gary was 19 when his car hit a lamppost in a busy street. Now he tells us why we should never speed in built-up areas.

'When I got my first car two weeks after passing my driving test, I thought I was brilliant. I felt as if I knew everything about cars and the roads, so I sometimes drove too fast and was not always fully in control of the car. Less than three weeks later I was seriously injured ...'

(WJEC Functional Skills English exam paper)

Text C is from an article in *The Daily Telegraph* by David Millward:

Recent statistics show one in five young drivers have an accident in the six months after passing their driving test. Transport ministers are examining the report which contains proposals intended to cut the number of young drivers involved in serious accidents. 15 per cent of the country's drivers are in their teens or twenties, but are involved in 34 per cent of crashes where injuries occur.

(WJEC English Language Foundation Paper, January 2015)

Text D is from an online news report:

Teens' Fundraising Marathon For Hospice Charity

Teenagers in Aylesbury have been very busy fundraising for a local hospice that's close to many of them.

The group of National Citizenship Service kids have chosen Helen and Douglas House as their charity project and have been in town today with a market stall to bring in the cash.

(online local news page, Aylesbury, August 2015)

Text E is an article from *The Telegraph*:

'Courageous' Stephen Sutton's fundraising legacy surpasses £5 million

The mother of Stephen Sutton, who charmed the nation with his selfless charity work, has said she is immensely proud as plans for the funds he raised are announced. It has been revealed that teenage cancer victim Stephen Sutton has raised over £5 million for the Teenage Cancer Trust charity.

www.thetelegraph.co.uk, 16/9/2014

Activity 3

You have been asked to take part in a talk show about teenage behaviour.

Take on the following roles in your group. You might like to include some anecdotes and examples in your discussion.

You are a **teenager** who has worked as a volunteer for local charities and you feel that teenagers have a lot to offer – providing they are shown the right direction.	You have **served a custodial sentence for drunken driving**. You have since reformed and gone back to school to resit your GCSEs. You believe that teenagers are unfairly treated. The issue is parenting and poor attitudes towards teenagers.
You are a **parent** who believes that teenagers have far too much leisure time. You feel that this leads to anti-social behaviour. You would like to argue for compulsory army experience for 16-year-olds.	You are a **teacher** and feel that teenagers have to grow up too quickly. You also feel that the media – and the internet – is responsible for influencing poor behaviour. What was once regarded as 'outrageous' is made 'normal' in the media.

Activity 4

In response to the letter from the resident, the headteacher has asked you to present your ideas on:

1 how people react to teenagers;

2 how we can improve teenagers' behaviour in the community.

Make your presentation to the headteacher and governors about the opinion of the school student council in response to the letter from a member of the public.

Here are some suggestions for achieving the success criteria:

- Organise information and ideas effectively and persuasively.
- Speak accurately and fluently.
- Express opinions with varied vocabulary and a range of techniques.
- Convey ideas clearly, precisely and appropriately.
- Support your ideas with examples.
- Use accurate grammar and a variety of sentence structures.

Reflect on these success criteria and your presentation by completing the table below. What are your targets for improvement?

Success criteria achieved	Targets for improvement

Stretch

For Activity 3, take the role of the talk show host. Try to skilfully 'balance' the talk so that a range of views are covered. Remember to sum up other people's viewpoints and ask more probing questions.

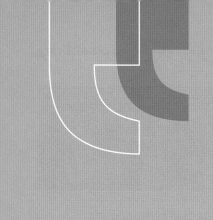

Reading

Learning objectives

In this unit you will be:
- retrieving and analysing information;
- analysing how effects are created;
- synthesising information.

Text A

'Don't Give Drink to Your Children'

Ban all alcohol until age of 15, says Chief Medical Officer

Children should not be given any alcohol before they turn 15, parents were told yesterday by Sir Liam Donaldson, the Government's Chief Medical Officer. He also warned parents that between the ages of 15 and 18 youngsters should drink no more than once a week, and then only under adult supervision. He made it clear that parents should monitor their children's alcohol intake, and set clear rules about when – and how much – they are allowed to drink. Parents should take a tough line if these rules are broken.

Sir Liam advised parents that letting their children have the occasional drink could be putting them at risk of brain damage, depression and memory problems. He explained that more than 10,000 children end up in hospital every year in England due to drinking, and research tells us that 15% of young people think it normal to get drunk once a week.

A series of guidelines has been written for parents by Sir Liam, which he hopes will assist in ensuring their children do not develop harmful and potentially dangerous drinking habits. Sir Liam says parents should lead by example and drink responsibly. Furthermore they should educate and inform children of the problems drinking can cause. He advised parents to make it clear to their children that getting drunk is not acceptable behaviour. It is important that parents provide their children with positive alternatives to drinking alcohol, such as playing sports or joining a club. Sir Liam also commented that parents should make it clear that a drunken teenager is neither macho nor amusing. He pointed to the real physical problems that alcohol could cause young people, such as liver damage and harm to the developing brain. It may also affect their emotions, lead to violent behaviour, and could cause memory loss.

Sir Liam explained that excessive drinking can lead to young people doing badly at school, and struggling to interact with friends and family. A report published earlier this year revealed that in the past four years 7,000 children had been permanently excluded from school, and a further 40,000 suspended, for alcohol and drug related incidents. It also stated that 4% of 15 to 16 year olds had been in trouble with the police through drinking.

(WJEC Functional Skills English exam paper)

Activity 5

Look at Text A:

1 What is the purpose of the text? Is it:
   a personal
   b public
   c educational
   d occupational?

2 Which three facts about the problem of teenage drinking are the most shocking?

3 Summarise, in your own words, Sir Liam Donaldson's advice to parents about alcohol and children.

Text B: Here are extracts from two blogs written by experts in response to Sir Liam Donaldson's advice.

I think Sir Liam Donaldson's advice is too black and white. In my opinion, it is the parents who know what's best for their own children, and allowing children to have alcohol is a decision for parents, not the Government.

Judith Reith, www. parentingpeople.co.uk

Sir Liam's advice is likely to make the problem worse and could lead to binge drinking, because children do not learn how to consume alcohol responsibly with their parents. Banning young children from drinking would only make them more curious about alcohol and therefore determined to try drinking.

Frank Furedi, Professor of Sociology

(WJEC Functional Skills English exam paper)

Activity 6

Look at Text B. Explain why Judith Reith and Frank Furedi disagree with Sir Liam Donaldson's views from Text A.

Activity 7

Text C is an article from *The Guardian* by Ellie Mae O'Hagan.

Last week, North Wales police joined forces with local councillors to turn Bangor's teenagers from loiterers into criminals. The city is now home to a curfew for its citizens under the age of 16. The curfew, or 'dispersal order' states: 'If you are under the age of 16 you are not allowed to be here between 9pm and 6am unless you are under the effective control of a parent or responsible person over the age of 18.' Those found breaking it could be fined up to £2,500, or even receive a custodial sentence.

Unsurprisingly, the move has been controversial; Keith Towler, the children's commissioner for Wales, says: 'It demonises under-16s, isolates them from their communities, alienates them from police and spreads the misconception all young people are troublemakers.'

www.theguardian.com, 2/7/2012

1 **Text C** uses the word 'controversial'. What is the nearest definition of the word?

a opposite

b contrary

c debatable

d annoying

2 Select a word from the list below to complete each of the following sentences.

Teenagers are often .... for .... behaviour because they hang around the streets at night. As a result it is .... to associate teenage with juvenile .... This, however, is a .... as crime .... tend to contradict this viewpoint. In fact the vast .... of teenagers are not involved in crime at all.

majority   criticised   easy   poor   crime   statistics   stereotype

Find a word which means:

a people who 'hang around';

b a regulation time limit;

c a type of punishment involving supervision by someone in authority;

d misunderstanding.

Read the following texts, which discuss the issue of young offenders, and answer the Test yourself question which follows.

Text D is an infographic.

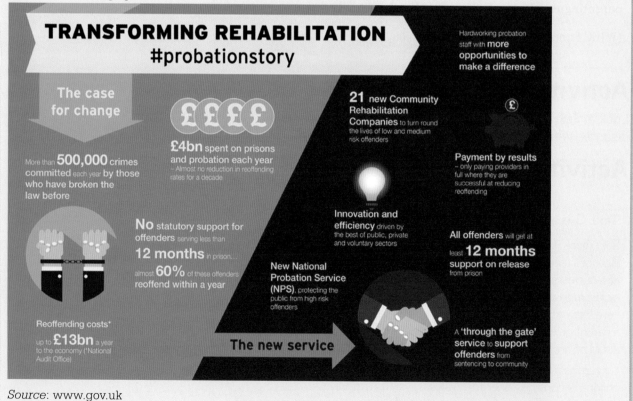

Source: www.gov.uk

Text E is a newspaper article.

Youth justice has change on the menu

The Government recently introduced a new sentence called a Youth Rehabilitation Order (YRO).This is a punishment, but it aims to help a young person stop committing crime by giving them expert training and job skills. This training will develop their skills and will benefit the local community.

This type of work is called reparation work, and gives youngsters a chance to make up for their bad behaviour by giving something to the community. If possible, reparation work should relate to the offence committed. For example, if a young person was guilty of graffiti, they may spend their time removing graffiti; or if they have broken windows in a youth club, they may have to help to paint and decorate the club. For some youngsters this can be very important, as it may make them feel less guilty for the upset and damage they have caused.

Another benefit of working in the local community is that it can help a young person get a job. There have been many examples of youngsters doing unpaid work as part of their punishment then obtaining a job because they have learned new skills and an ability to work hard. Oldham Youth Offending Service has been sending groups of young offenders to work on a gardening allotment. Bob Anderson, Chairman of the Allotment Association, explained that young offenders, both boys and girls, have grown vegetables, pruned trees and made a pond.

Mr. Anderson doesn't think that the young people see working on an allotment as an easy option. He said: 'They find it hard work, which they have to do in all weathers. They are out in the fresh air rather than locked up, and are not mixing with hardened criminals, or learning bad habits. They're here doing something constructive. They see what their work is achieving, which makes them happy. It's hard work, but they go away better people than when they started the work. Young people gain self-esteem, pride in their work, and respect for others. By growing plants they can see the results of their hard work. This type of scheme really does give young offenders the chance to turn their lives around.'

Dave, aged 17, had twice been arrested for shoplifting. Part of his sentence was to repair old bicycles and sell them for charity. He found the work really enjoyable, made friends with fellow workers, and learned practical skills. He now has a full-time job repairing bicycles, and his life has improved in many ways. He says: 'At first I was angry that I was expected to work for nothing, but to be honest I loved it and it has changed my life.'

(Adapted from *The Manchester Evening News*)

Test yourself

How do Texts D and E support the idea that 'prevention is better than cure'? [10]

Top tips

This question asks you to look at BOTH texts but isn't asking you to **compare** the texts. You have to focus on two skills here: **synthesis** (looking at more than one text) and **analysis** (how the articles present information). It is very important to refer to a range of evidence in both texts and get the focus of your answer right. As the language is not persuasive or figurative it is sometimes difficult to spot 'technique' in texts like this. Use the box shown here to help you.

Technique	Text D	Text E	Both
Opinions			
Factual examples			
Positive language			
Case studies			
Interview			
Images			
Statistics			

Stretch

What reading strategies have you used in this section of the unit for these reading skills? Copy and complete the table below.

Find some continuous and non-continuous texts that present information about different aspects of teenage behaviour. Explain how these texts are different.

Activity	Strategy
Purpose of a text	
Evaluating	
Summarising	
Synthesising	
Locating information	
Analysing	

Writing

Activity 8 Test your accuracy

This letter about raising the legal driving age has been sent to a newspaper, but the editor must correct errors in spelling, punctuation and grammar before it can be published. Identify and correct the errors.

Dear editor, im wrighting you a letter about the age limit going up to 19 because of all the accidents they all have. Teenagers 17 to 18 should still be able to drive if they payed for there insurance they are covered about. 45% of 17 to 18 years olds drive fast and play loud music and the other 55% drive sensaball so that not fair on the people who do drive with care around the strrets. 17 to 18 years olds start getting jobs and most of them may need a car to get to work or maybe thay need to be able to drive to there jobs. You should leave the age limit as they are and as long there psying the tax and insurance there no problem. Yours senscelly.

Activity 9

Read the following paragraph written by a student.

People think that footballers are the role models for the teenagers of today. I think this idea is wrong because often footballers are guilty of behaving badly on the football field. Footballers clearly think that it isn't wrong to spit, argue, cheat and disrespect officials even though teenagers are watching them on television and they might decide to copy their footballing heroes. I think something needs to be done before youngsters lose all sense of what it means to be a good role model.

The student shows a sensible viewpoint here but the ideas sound repetitive.

1 What words or phrases are repeated?
2 Can you think of any synonyms to replace these words? It may be useful to use a thesaurus to help you with your choices.
3 Now improve this paragraph by using a wider variety of words and phrases.

Top tips

- Are there any clues in the use of connectives to help you make your decision?
- Are there any paragraphs about similar topics that might go next to each other?

Activity 10 Paragraphing

Here is a speech about the disadvantages of mobile phones. The paragraphs are well written but they are a bit jumbled, so the writer's argument does not sound well organised. Read the speech and decide the order in which the paragraphs should be written so that the writer's ideas connect more logically.

Only last week in our own high street, ladies and gentlemen, a young mother was viciously mugged in broad daylight when she used her mobile to call a taxi. Surely we cannot allow this sort of appalling crime to continue?

Furthermore, mobiles are causing chaos in schools. They disturb lessons and have actually been used by dishonest pupils to help them cheat in exams!

Teenagers are stealing and shoplifting more than ever to pay their mobile phone bills. Even the Prime Minister admitted last week that he himself was very worried about how much money his own children were wasting on 'mindlesss mobile chat'.

In conclusion, I know the listeners to this programme are more intelligent people who will be just as worried about these microwave monsters as I am. I admit they can be useful in emergencies, but how often do these really happen? Meanwhile our young people are causing serious damage to the most important and delicate part of their bodies.

We have managed perfectly well without mobile phones in the past, and I strongly believe that when the real facts about them are known, we will have to cope without them in the future because they will be banned!

Thank you for listening and goodnight.

Text messaging is also causing serious problems in schools because youngsters become so used to writing in this shorthand style that they forget how to write properly and fail their GCSEs. Do we really want a younger generation who can only scrawl in meaningless slang?

Activity 11

A paragraph is a series of sentences about the same topic or which follow on from each other.

You should use paragraphs to divide and organise your ideas. Paragraphs help your readers follow your train of thought; this will be especially important when you are trying to build a clear and logical argument.

Write four paragraph starters giving your viewpoint on one of these statements:

Going to the zoo encourages cruelty to animals.

Wearing a hoody 'up' in public is antisocial.

You may want to use some of these linking words (connectives) to help link your paragraphs, or think of some of your own.

also	*too*	*however*	*besides*
firstly	*secondly*	*moreover*	*then*
finally	*likewise*	*next*	*in a nutshell*
to sum up	*in addition to*	*consequently*	*as a result*
since	*nevertheless*		

Stretch

Using your partner's paragraph starters, complete four paragraphs on the chosen statement.

Test yourself

Read the following exam-style question carefully:

'Rude, idle hooligans who intimidate passers-by and loiter on street corners.'

Write an essay explaining how you would encourage older people to think differently about teenagers. [35]

As with all the other extended writing tasks in this book, it is important to PLAN your response. Write down a list of ideas or points you might want to include in your essay.

Here are some sentence starters you might find useful to help link your paragraphs together:

In my view/opinion …

I believe/I feel …

I feel strongly that …

The evidence points to …

It is obvious that …

Overall, I believe/I am of the opinion that …

There is no doubt that …

And some starters for counter-argument:

Many people believe that …

An alternative view is …

While some people suggest, the facts …

However, this is clearly not the case …

This is far from the truth …

After looking at the evidence, it is clear …

Top tips

This is an expository essay which is asking you to **explain** your ideas. The previous reading section had lots of examples of expository writing and it is worth reviewing these before you start to write. The following elements can be used to sustain your writing:

1 Opinions – this includes your own opinions as well as others' views.
2 Factual examples – support your ideas with statistics.
3 Counter-argument – purposely bring in an opposing view only to give reasons against it.
4 Case studies – this can be an anecdote from your experience.
5 Interview – you could do this using direct speech.

Sample student responses

Which of the following **openings** are most focused on the brief given in the exam question?

Answer 1

I believe that teenagers should get out in the community more and actively help those people in most need. The best way of doing this would be to join up for a local charity fundraiser and give up your time to improve the situations of people who are less fortunate than you. Teenagers should stop wasting their time and money drinking and smoking by bus-stops and start making a positive difference to others. I would recommend the following actions:

1 Do more volunteering;

2 Take up more exercise;

3 Spend more time on school work.

Volunteering

There are lots of fantastic charities around and I would recommend starting by looking at the following website …

Answer 2

I know that we might seem to be an intimidating bunch but we really are not as horrible as we look! I believe that you 'oldies' need to think differently about young people as we really do have loads to offer and it's not fair to say we're a bunch of loud yobs who waste time on street corners and bus stops. Some of my best friends have done wonders for other people …

Match up the comment below to Answer 1 or 2:
Examiner comment:

While this is a structured and methodical opening, this is the wrong focus. The question makes it clear that the audience is 'older people' who have a negative view of teenagers. The task gives advice and is **persuasive** rather than **expository** (writing to explain).

Stretch

Write a comment on the 'other' answer. There is one positive aspect here – but also a few 'points for action'. Can you spot these?

Busting the jargon

AO2 – Reading tasks

Lower tariff reading questions – these feature throughout the book:

Retrieve (*Find... Identify...*)

Verbal reasoning (*Which word...*)

Bias/reliability/facts

Collate (*Find... Select...*).

Higher tariff reading questions. These feature on the page numbers given. There is guidance for completion of these in the Student book and Teacher book:

Summarise (*Sum up... What are the main ...*) pp. 29, 130

Synthesise (*Look at both texts...*) pp.10, 77, 108, 166

Infer/deduce (*What impressions...*) pp.19, 87, 110

Analyse (*How does the writer...*) pp. 53, 98, 120, 143, 154

Interpret (*What attitudes...*) pp. 64, 131

Evaluate (*What thoughts/feelings...*) pp. 27, 154

Reflect/assess (*What do you think of...*) pp. 29, 41

Explain (*Explain...Why does...*) pp. 64, 77, 131

Compare/contrast (*Compare both...*) pp. 66, 132

AO3 – Written tasks

These can take a range of text formats. For example, an 'account' may take a narrative or descriptive form. As a result, a range of formats with more specific guidance are included throughout the textbook on the page numbers given:

Narrative – these are different from descriptions as there is a **clear sense of action**, **character** (avoid too many), and **structure** (it should have a beginning, middle and end). Examples of narratives might be a story, accounts of personal experiences or a report. These appear on pages 33 and 125.

Descriptive – these describe events, places, actions and feelings. This form of writing may take various formats, e.g. travel writing, diaries or accounts of personal experiences. These appear on pages 69 and 101.

Exposition – these explain your personal views on a topic. Examples may include an essay, a letter or an article. These appear on pages 90, 113, 136 and 169.

Argumentation – these present a view of a topic, although you can take more than one viewpoint on the topic. Examples may include a report, letter or article. These appear on pages 14, 57, 81 and 158.

Persuasive – these aim to convince the reader of the writer's viewpoint and may appeal to the reader's emotions in a personal way. Examples may include a letter, speech or review. These appear on pages 23, 44, 147.

Proofreading – this is a task where you will have to find errors in a text. These appear on pages 13, 23, 30, 43, 55, 67, 81, 89, 101, 111, 122, 134, 144 and 167.

Text level

For your GCSE study, you need to know four broad purposes or 'contexts' for reading:

- personal;
- public;
- occupational;
- educational.

Personal texts satisfy a reader's personal interests – these also includes texts which have a personal connection to other people, such as letters.

Public texts relate to activities and concerns of society as a whole – these could include information about public events and official documents.

Occupational texts refer to reading which has to be done as part of a job role. These are usually linked to immediate tasks, such as searching for a job.

Educational texts encourage learning or instruction – best summarised as 'reading to learn'.

Copy and complete the table below, placing these texts in the most appropriate box:

1 Letter written to an aunt in your family.
2 A cookery recipe.
3 News website featuring national stories.
4 A novel written by Jacqueline Wilson.
5 Health and safety rules at your new job.
6 Interactive website teaching you how to play piano.
7 Fire drill instructions at place of work.
8 Forum blog based on charity for refugees.

Personal	Public	Occupational	Educational

Texts can also be **continuous** or **non-continuous**. Continuous texts follow a logical sequence and rely on the order of reading to make sense of it, e.g. a recipe or novel. A non-continuous text does not rely on this order and will have elements of required information in different places, e.g. a website, a television guide.

Finally, the exam will test your ability to write in the following styles: narrative, description, argumentation, persuasive, expository.

- **Narrative** refers to a chain of actions or events, e.g. stories, accounts of personal experiences or diary entries.
- **Description** refers to writing which focuses on describing a situation or context, e.g. describe a time when you felt scared.
- **Argumentation** refers to writing where you are putting forward an **argument** or **viewpoint,** e.g. formal letter.
- **Persuasive** refers to writing which tries to **persuade** the reader, e.g. speech or advertisement for a charity.
- **Expository** writing refers to writing which **explains** a viewpoint or issue, e.g. study guide, essay or report which explains how to improve the environment.

Sentence level

A 'normal' sentence should have a subject and verb, e.g.

The dog barked at the strange man across the road.

- 'The dog' is the subject and 'barked' is the verb.

She is a world-famous cook.

- 'She' is the subject and 'is' is the verb.

There are four types of sentences:
- minor;
- simple;
- compound;
- complex.

A **minor** sentence breaks grammar rules as there is a subject or verb (or both!) missing, e.g. 'The painting. Laughter.'

A **simple sentence** has only one subject and verb. These are two simple sentences, e.g. 'I looked at the painting. I laughed at it.'

A **compound sentence** connects two or more simple clauses or sentences using the conjunctions 'and', 'or', 'but', 'so', 'or' (these are the conjunctions you should **avoid** starting a sentence with), e.g. 'I looked at the painting *and* I laughed at it.'

A **complex sentence** connects clauses with a subordinating conjunction. Complex sentences imply that one clause is more important, and they can be moved around so that the subordinating conjunction can move to the front of the sentences, e.g. 'I laughed while I looked at the painting.', 'While I looked at the painting I started laughing.'

Copy and complete the table below, placing these sentences into the right table. **Hint:** the use of conjunctions will help you identify the sentence type:

1 Whenever I run long distances, my arm starts shaking.
2 Double trouble.
3 The lady in the blue coat walked across the main road by herself.
4 The man crossed the road and stopped on the other side.
5 However angry you feel right now, time will help you get it into perspective.
6 I threw the ball in the air and caught it with my foot.
7 Time and time again.
8 Time stopped.

Minor sentence	Simple sentence	Compound sentence	Complex sentence

Sentence functions

There are four **functions** of sentences:

- statements (declaratives);
- imperatives;
- questions (interrogatives);
- exclamatives.

Statements are the most commonly used sentences – these can either be statements that sound factual (e.g. They are the most efficient), give opinions (e.g. I think they're great) or they can describe actions or events (e.g. They climbed Everest).

Imperatives are commands and they start with the verb itself, e.g. 'Calm down', 'Stand up.' Negative imperatives start with the helping (auxiliary) verb 'don't', e.g. 'Don't shout.'

Questions will always end with a question mark (?). Sometimes they serve a function, e.g. 'What time is it?' Sometimes they can be rhetorical (for effect), e.g. 'Why do we always make the same mistake?'

Exclamatives end with exclamation marks and liven up writing' e.g. 'What a day!'

Copy and complete the table below, placing these sentences into the right column:

1 Where are the highest mountain peaks in the world?
2 Turn left after the roundabout.
3 He was unspeakably rude!
4 Nine out of ten cats prefer dog food.

5 Why do eyes twitch just before we go to sleep?

6 The longest river in the world is in South America.

7 Place two teaspoons of sugar in the bowl.

8 No way am I going there!

Statement	Imperative	Question	Exclamative

Word level Nouns

Nouns are labels for things, ideas, or people. These are two main types of nouns: proper nouns and common nouns.

Proper nouns are labels for specific people, places or events, e.g. Waterloo, Matt Smith.

Common nouns can be separated into three 'sub-types' – concrete, abstract and collective nouns:

- **Concrete nouns** are labels for things that can be seen or touched, e.g. table, ball.
- **Abstract nouns** are labels for feelings or ideas (things that cannot be seen or touched), e.g. happiness, solitude.
- **Collective nouns** are names for groups of things, e.g. a herd of sheep, a pack of lions.

Being creative with nouns:

1 Personifying abstract nouns can be effective in stories, e.g. 'Silence came into the room.' Have a go at starting a sentence with these abstract nouns: loneliness, hunger, joy.

2 You can make abstract nouns out of the of adjectives, e.g. lonely – loneliness. Can you make abstract nouns out of these adjectives?:

hungry *tragic* *attractive* *clever* *stupid*

funny *joyful* *civilised* *painful* *long*

3 Collective nouns are fun if you make them up, e.g. a muttering of children. Make up some collective nouns for these plural nouns:

teachers *shoppers* *toys* *paper-clips*

4 Copy and complete the table below, sorting out these nouns into their 'types':

cow *magic* *Mr Gordon* *bus* *World War II*

clock *platoon* *boredom* *key* *Paris*

sight *assortment* *thumb* *Cardiff* *love*

Proper	Concrete	Abstract	Collective

Stretch
Use all of the words opposite for either:
- an advertisement for a holiday; or
- an opening paragraph of a horror or fantasy story.

Adjectives

Adjectives describe or modify a noun. They either **tell us more** about the noun (e.g. the **green** room), or about the **attitude** shown towards the noun (e.g. the **most fantastic** opportunity).

Broadly speaking, there are two types of adjectives:
- factual;
- evaluative.

Factual adjectives give basic information about the noun that is not a matter of opinion, e.g. green room, round table, miniscule grain of sand.

Evaluative adjectives make a 'value judgement' about the noun, e.g. the most boring experience, tragic consequence, a bright student. Evaluative adjectives can sometimes be emotive – they are used to stir emotions in people and can be used in persuasive writing very effectively.

As evaluative adjectives reveal emotions to the reader, writers try to avoid **over-using** these in stories as they **tell** the reader instead of **showing**. Factual adjectives can sometimes work better as the reader can make up their own mind in narrative writing.

1 Identify the **evaluative** adjectives in the passage below.

2 Turn them into **factual** adjectives. How does this affect the writing?

    The scary man opened his mouth and a really awful scream came out. His hideous clothes clung tightly to his arms. A horrific hand appeared out of his shirt cuff and pointed at me. A creepy smile hung on his lips as he spoke.

3 In addition, adjectives can be **superlative** (e.g. greatest, most wonderful) or **comparative** (e.g. greater, more wonderful). Copy and complete the table below, turning these adjectives into superlative and comparative adjectives. What patterns do you notice?

    bad   hungry   quick   beautiful   green   terrific

Adjective	Comparative	Superlative

Verbs

Verbs or verb phrases act like the muscles of a sentence. They can either be doing verbs (**dynamic**) or simply state things (**stative**). Which are **stative** or **dynamic** in the sentences below?

1 They **are** very late today.

2 The cat **jumped** on the table.

3   This programme **is** the best.

4   You **seem** a bit irritable at the moment.

5   The spider **fell down** the plug-hole.

6   I **stopped** the bus just in time.

Verbs are very important in your own writing as they can help to show your ambition. A well-chosen verb can help to make your writing more figurative. For example:

- 'The trees **shook** in the wind' sounds quite effective; but
- 'The trees **quivered** in the wind' helps to personify the trees and 'lifts' the quality of your writing.

Use any of the verbs in the table below to help with the concrete nouns opposite:

Verb	Noun
Roared Stammered Stampeded	Smoke Flames Students

Tenses

Verbs can be in a range of tenses. It is very important to be consistent in your use of tenses in writing as it is easy to slip out of tense. Spot the errors in tense below:

It is Christmas morning and I see a massive snowman outside my window. I look out and it is silent and beautiful.

I jumped out of bed and shouted:

'Yippee!'

When I ran down the stairs I see it all before my eyes. The tree is fallen over and my presents have been torn apart.

Adverbs

Adverbs modify a verb in a similar way to how adjectives modify nouns: e.g. silent (adjective) night (noun); but silently (adverb) move (verb).

They can often be formed by taking an adjective and adding -ly to the end. Change the following adjectives into adverbs:

beautiful   quick   hungry   tragic

(Adjectives 3 and 4 are more awkward to spell – how do you alter the spelling to suit?)

Adverbs (like adjectives) can also reveal the attitude of the writer about what is being said, and this can often be a feature of argumentation or persuasive writing: e.g. unfortunately, reluctantly, gladly, understandably.

These can be very useful as sentence starters in more formal writing.

Other word classes

There are four other small word classes – these are sometimes referred to as 'function' words as they help the main word classes to function more smoothly in texts. These are:

- pronouns;
- prepositions;
- determiners;
- conjunctions.

The most useful function words for your study of English Language are **pronouns** and **conjunctions**.

As mentioned on page 173, **conjunctions** are 'joining words'. They are needed for creating complex and compound sentences.

Pronouns are small words which replace a noun. These are usually: I, you, he, she, it (singular form); we, you, they (plural form).

Figurative features

Figurative features are another way of 'viewing' or 'reading' words and phrases. These are words used for 'effect'.

Simile: a comparison which explains the basis of the resemblance, e.g. 'Usain Bolt **was as quick as** lightning.'

Metaphor: a comparison which does not reveal the basis of the resemblance – this makes them more complex to work out, e.g. 'She was a bolt of lightning.' Metaphor also encompasses **personification** and **imagery**.

Personification: when an inanimate object is given human or living qualities, e.g. 'The traffic lights winked at me.' Personification is easily created by using more unusual **verbs**.

Imagery: this is a general term for figurative writing which creates a strong image for the reader, e.g. 'The lake was a sliver of gold and silver under a grey sky.'

Alliteration: the use of repeated letter sounds to create a memorable effect or easier articulation, e.g.' The **n**ail was **kn**ocked through the **gn**arled wood.'

Onomatopoeia: sound words, e.g. 'The wasps **buzzed**.'

Oxymoron: words or phrases that appear to contradict each other, e.g. 'The boy let out a **silent scream**.'

Hyperbole: exaggeration for emphasis, e.g. '**For the millionth time** ...'

Pun: wordplay on a phrase or word that has two meanings, e.g. 'I wondered why the ball got bigger. Then it **hit** me.'

How many features can you spot in the description below?

> *The trees arched over me slowly and seemed to shove me in the direction of the building. I tiptoed towards the terror that awaited. The windows seemed to be darker than the pit of hell and when*

I rapped on the door my knuckles gathered a smooth splinter. I yelped in pain. Suddenly the door opened.

I had finally arrived at the dentist.

'Please take a seat,' the receptionist said.

I smiled at her. I knew the drill.

Continue this piece, describing the painful experience in the chair. Try to make use of at least four well-chosen figures of speech.

The skills of reading

More functional skills	More complex skills
Retrieve (*Find … Identify …*) Verbal reasoning (*Which word …*) Bias/reliability/facts Summarise (*Sum up …What are the main …*) Collate (*Find … Select …*) Synthesise (*Look at both texts …*)	Infer/deduce (*What impressions …*) Analyse (*How does the writer …*) Interpret (*What attitudes …*) Evaluate (*What thoughts/feelings …*) Reflect/assess Explain (*Explain… Why does …*) Compare/contrast (*Compare both …*)

The new English Language specification will test the full range of skills above. It is useful to identify which skills a question may test. In some questions it may test more than one skill.

Spot the skills tested in the questions below:

1 Identify two challenges faced by the company. (2)

2 Both texts are about marathon-running. Compare their attitudes to training and other competitors. (10)

3 Circle the word that best fills the gap:

Geological shift is a _____ process

tough   slow-moving   boring   splendid (1)

4 How does the writer present Cardiff in the extract? (5)

5 What impressions do you get of the Formula One driver? How does the writer create these impressions? (10)

6 How did Paula O'Connell feel when she won the gold medal? (5)

7 Which two countries produce the most oil (after reading the text)? (2)

8 Explain how mobile phones became must-have accessories in 'the noughties'. (5)

9 What does the writer feel about whale-fishing? (10)

The marks in brackets are also a clue about the expected amount to be written. Which are the three easiest questions? Which are the three toughest questions?

Acknowledgements

The Publishers would like to thank the following for permission to reproduce copyright material.

Photo credits: p.5 © Gail Johnson – Fotolia; **p.6** © Bahadir Yeniceri – Thinkstock/Getty Images; **p.9** © Andres Rodriguez – Fotolia; **p.14** © FrankieCarr – Thinkstock/Getty Images; **p.16** © Ivary – Thinkstock/Getty Images; **p.21** © Sergey Peterman – Getty Images; **p.23 (1st, right)** © C Squared Studios – Photodisc/Getty Images, **(2nd, right)** © Stockbyte/Getty Images, **(3rd, right)** © Design Pics – Thinkstock/Getty Images; **p.24 (top)** © Richard Levine/Alamy Stock Photo; **p.24 (middle)** © True Images/Alamy Stock Photo; **p.27** © Hulton Archive/Stringer – Getty Images; **p.30** © Photodisc – Thinkstock/Getty Images; **p.32 (top)** © Elaineitalia – Thinkstock/Getty Images; **p.32 (middle)** © fotokostic – Thinkstock/Getty Images; **p.34** © LifesizeImages – Thinkstock/Getty Images; **p.35** © dolgachov – iStock via Thinkstock/Getty Images; **p.38 (top)** © Folly Farm Adventure Park and Zoo, Pembrokeshire (www.folly-farm.co.uk); **p.39** © kzenon- Thinkstock/Getty Images; **p.46** © ventdusud – Thinkstock/Getty Images; **p.47** © mroz – Thinkstock/Getty Images; **p.49** © Infographic by www.AlphaHolidayLettings.com; **p.50** © Brian Jackson – Thinkstock/Getty Images; **p.53** © Tracy Gunn/Alamy Stock Photo; **p.58** © LiubovTerletska – Thinkstock/Getty Images; **p.59** © monkeybusinessimages – Thinkstock/Getty Images; **p.65** © News Creative/Alamy Stock Photo; **p.67** © wavebreakmedia Ltd – Thinkstock/Getty Images; **p.72** © LuminaStock – Thinkstock/Getty Images; **p.73** © monkeybusinessimages – Thinkstock/Getty Images; **p.78** © Jose Luis Pelaez Inc – Thinkstock/Getty Images; **p.84** © Purestock – Thinkstock/Getty Images; **p.85** © Skye Gould/Business Insider; **p.89** © Bibigon – Thinkstock/Getty Images; **p.92 (1st, top)** © Michelle Kays, **(2nd, top)** © Via www.mindwerx.com, **(3rd, top)** © REEF ®, **(4th, top)** © WoofWasher.com, **(5th, top)** © Stockbyte/ Getty Images Ltd/ Fast Food SD175; **p.97** © Sylphe_7 – Thinkstock/Getty Images; **p.99** © Tomwang112 – Thinkstock/Getty Images; **p.101** © pterwort – Thinkstock/Getty Images; **p.104 (bottom)** © George Doyle – Stockbyte/Thinkstock Getty Images; **p.106** © Thomas Northcut – Thinkstock/Getty Images; **p.109** © John Stillwell/WPA Pool/Getty Images; **p.113** © JACK TAYLOR/AFP/Getty Images; **p.115** © moodboard – Thinkstock/Getty Images; **p.116** © monkeybusinessimages – Thinkstock/Getty Images; **p.117** © derdy – fotolia; **p.119** © Jetta Productions – Thinkstock/Getty Images; **p.122** © johnnorth – Thinkstock/Getty Images; **p.127** © Ingram Publishing – Thinkstock/Getty Images; **p.129** © tupungato – Thinkstock/Getty Images; **p.132** © Simon Dawson/Bloomberg via Getty Images; **p.135** © ikImages/REX Shutterstock; **p.136** © dejanj01 – Thinkstock/Getty Images; **p.137** © mangostock – Thinkstock/Getty Images; **p.140** © Studio-Annika – Thinkstock/Getty Images; **p.141** © Bozidar Vukicevic/SIPA/REX Shutterstock; **p.142** © Save the Children; **p.144 (top)** © Jacob Ammentorp Lund – Thinkstock/Getty Images; **p.145** © Fuse – Thinkstock/Getty Images; **p.148 (top)** © monkeybusinessimages – Thinkstock/Getty Images, **(middle)** © Jupiterimages – Thinkstock/Getty Images; **p.149** © Highwaystarz-Photography – Thinkstock/Getty Images; **p.150** © Realimage/Alamy Stock Photo; **p.152** © Infographic by Kathryn Watson © The Scout Association; **p.155** © Fuse – Thinkstock/Getty Images; **p.157** © T.M.O.Travel/Alamy Stock Photo; **p.159** © Jupiterimages – Thinkstock/Getty Images; **p.161** © Highwaystarz-Photography – Thinkstock/Getty Images; **p.162** © Design pics – Thinkstock/Getty Images; **p.164** © Open Government Licence; **p.165** © Stu/Alamy Stock Photo; **p.168** © Roadknight – Fotolia.

Text acknowledgements: p.5: **Author unknown:** 'Welcome to Laguna Health & spa, Cardiff', from www.lagunahealthandspa.com (2009); **p.7 (top left): Author unknown:** from http://journeyplanner.rugbyworldcup.com/#/; **p.7 (top right): Author unknown:** 'Bring the kids along to our Soft Play Shack', from https://surfsnowdonia.co.uk/bring-the-kids-along-to-our-soft-play-shack/ (30 July); **p.7 (bottom left): Author unknown:** 'How to Surf', from www.wikihow.com/Surf; **p.7 (bottom right): Author unknown:** 'Wales, the home of coasteering', from www.visitwales.com/things-to-do/activities/watersports/coasteering/guide-to-coasteering; **p.10 (top): Author unknown:** 'Family fun', from www.cardiffcastle.com/family-fun/; **p.10 (bottom): Author unknown:** 'Cardiff Castle', from www.visitwales.com/attraction-search/attraction-search-results/attraction-search-details?id=516060; **p.17: Carrie Evans:** from http://www.walesonline.co.uk/news/wales-news/residents-town-hit-comedy-stella-6799611 (2014), © 2016 Media Wales Ltd; **p.18 (top): DTZ:** 'Economic impact of S4C: Final report', from www.s4c.cymru/abouts4c/corporate/pdf/s4c_economic_report_2010.pdf (2010); **p.18 (bottom): Martin Shipton:** 'Viewing figures of S4C do not justify its continued existence, says former minister', from www.walesonline.co.uk/news/wales-news/viewing-figures-s4c-not-justify-1938953 (2010); **p.19: Author unknown:** 'Interview: Ed Thomas, Hinterland/Y Gwyll', from https://thekillingtimestv.wordpress.com/2015/09/17/interview-ed-thomas-hinterlandy-gwyll/ (2015);

p.26: Welsh Government: from http://gov.wales/docs/statistics/2015/ (2015), Intellectual Property Office © Crown copyright 2015; **p.27 (top): Welsh Government:** from http://gov.wales/docs/statistics/2015/150914-national-survey-wales-2014-15-headline-results-revised-en.pdf (2015), Intellectual Property Office © Crown copyright 2015; **p.27 (bottom) and p.28: Dylan Thomas:** from *Portrait of the Artist as a Young Dog* (New Directions Publishing, 1968), From Thomas, D. (1968) A Portrait of the Artist as a Young Dog by New Directions Publishing; **p.34: Author unknown** from http://www.valekarate.com (year), © Vale Karate; **p.35 (top): Author unknown:** from http://www.visitwales.com/things-to-do/activities/watersports/windsurfing (Visit Wales, 2015), Intellectual Property Office © Crown copyright 2015; **p.35 (middle): Author unknown:** from http://www.nickypalmerfitness.co.uk/what-to-expect/ (Nicky Palmer Fitness, 2015), Copyright © 2015 Nicky Palmer Fitness; **p.35 (bottom): Author unknown:** from http://www.leisurecentre.com/cardiff-international-pool/Activity/childrens-swimming-lessons (Parkwood Leisure Limited, 2014), Parkwood Leisure Limited © Copyright 2014; **p.37: Christian Michener:** from *Numerology* (New Rivers Press, 2006), From Michener, C. (2006) 'Numerology' by New Rivers Press; **p.39: Author unknown:** from https://www.healthychildren.org (American Academy of Pediatrics, 2016), Copyright © American Academy of Pediatrics; **p.40 (top): Author unknown:** from http://www.findingmyfitness.com (2016), Copyright © Finding My Fitness; **p.40 (bottom): Lauren Brown, Sam Webb:** from http://www.mirror.co.uk/news/uk-news/pe-letter-mum-family-reveal-5368152 (MGN Limited, 2016), © Mirrorpix; **p.42: Philip Dewey:** from http://www.walesonline.co.uk/news/wales-news/chris-thomas-ironman-tenby-diet-9982392 (2015), © Trinity Mirror Publishing; **p.46 (left): Author unknown:** from http://www.thomson.co.uk/destinations/the-americas/united-states-of-america/florida/holidays-florida.html (TUI Group, 2016), © 2015 TUI UK; **p.46 (right): Author unknown:** from http://www.queenstownnz.co.nz/#sthash.p7iQ01Sw.dpuf (Destination Queenstown, 2016), © Copyright 2016 Destination Queenstown; **p.47 (left): Author unknown:** from http://www.travelsupermarket.com/c/holidays/australia/sydney/87/ (Moneysupermarket Financial Group, 2016), © MoneySuperMarket.com Limited; **p.47 (right): Author unknown:** from http://www.kuoni.co.uk/hong-kong (Kuoni Travel, 2016), ©2016 Kuoni Travel; **p.47 (bottom): Author unknown:** from http://www.travelsupermarket.com/c/holidays/thailand/koh-samui/95/ (Moneysupermarket Financial Group, 2016), © MoneySuperMarket.com Limited; **p.50 (left): Nigel H. Jones:** from *Tower: An Epic History of the Tower of London* (Random House Publishing, 2011), From *Tower* by Nigel Jones, published by Hutchinson. Reproduced by permission of The Random House Group Ltd.; **p.50 (right): Author unknown:** from http://www.londontravelwatch.org.uk/consumer_advice/money_saving_transport_tips (2016), © Copyright London TravelWatch 2016; **p.50 (bottom): Author unknown:** from http://www.tripadvisor.co.uk, © 2016 TripAdvisor LLC All rights reserved; **p.51: Sarah Gordon:** from http://www.dailymail.co.uk/travel/article-2599602/London-vs-Paris-battle-tourists-The-graphic-compares-two-capitals.html#ixzz3k88b2pNr (2014), London vs Paris: The infographic that puts the two capitals head-to-head in their battle for supremacy by Sarah Gordon. © Daily Mail. Used by permission; **p.53: Author unknown:** from http://www.thedungeons.com/london/en/ (2016), © Copyright 2016 Merlin Entertainments; **p.62: Andrew Trendell:** text from http://www.gigwise.com/news/91704/new-infographic-reveals-how-much-glastonbury-actually-costs (2014), Copyright © 2016 GIGWISE Ltd.; **p.65 (top): Louise Tickle:** from 'Music festivals: the sound of escapism', http://www.theguardian.com/education/2011/jul/18/music-festivals-research (*The Guardian Online*, 2011), Copyright Guardian News & Media Ltd 2016; **p.65 (bottom): Tony Naylor:** from 'Music festivals: why do we do it?, http://www.theguardian.com/music/musicblog/2008/jun/23/ihatefestivals (*The Guardian Online*, 2008), Copyright Guardian News & Media Ltd 2016; **p.74: Madhumita Murgia:** from 'Technology in classrooms doesn't make students smarter', http://www.telegraph.co.uk/technology/news/11865605/Technology-in-classrooms-doesnt-make-students-smarter.html (The Telegraph, 2015), © Telegraph Media Group Limited 2015; **p.75: Discussion in 'Behaviour' started by joedoggyuk:** from https://community.tes.com/threads/mobile-phone-jammers.717198/#post-8724051 (TES, 2015), © TES Global Ltd; **p.85 (top): Author unknown:** from http://scarc.library.oregonstate.edu/coll/pauling/peace/notes/safe4.037-118.html (2015), Courtesy Ava Helen and Linus Pauling's papers, Oregon State University Libraries; **p.86 (left): Rob Horlock:** from *I Remember When I Was Young* (Unlimited Publishing, 2014), I Remember When I Was Young by Rob Horlock © Unlimited Publishing; **p.86 (right): Robert Crampton:** from http://www.thetimes.co.uk/tto/magazine/article3883918.ece (2013), © Times Newspapers Limited; **p.94: Hubert H. Humphrey:** from *The Futurist* (World Future Society, 1967), © The Futurist magazine; **p.95: Author unknown:** from http://csglobe.com/the-10-biggest-dangers-posed-by-future-technology/ (2015), © CSGlobe; **p.97: Isaac Asimov:** from *I, Robot* (Harper Collins, 2013), I, Robot by Isaac Asimov by permission of HarperCollins; **p.107 (left): Emily Dugan:** from http://www.independent.co.uk/news/uk/home-news/more-women-have-jobs-in-britain-than-ever-before-but-figures-show-the-gender-pay-gap-is-rising-too-9139154.html (2014), © The Independent, **(right): Tim Lambert:** from http://www.localhistories.org/womensjobs.html (2016), Used by permission from Tim Lambert; **p.108: Author unknown:** from https://www.worldpayzinc.com/attitudes-in-the-workplace.pdf (2015), © 2015 WorldPay (UK) Limited; **p.109: Author unknown:** from http://www.rbs-businesssense.co.uk/Karen-brady2.html (2011), © Royal Bank of Scotland;

p.113: Author unknown: from www.royalnavy.mod.uk/brochure (2015), © Crown Copyright 2015 Royal Navy; **p.115 (Text 1): Author unknown:** from http://www.futuremorph.org/14-16/work-experience, © Future Morph; **(Text 3): Charlie Mayfield:** from http://www.telegraph.co.uk/finance/jobs/youth-unemployment-competition/9656587/What-young-people-need-more-than-anything-is-work-experience.html (2012), © Telegraph Media Group Limited 2012; **p.116 (Text 4): Author unknown:** from http://webarchive.nationalarchives.gov.uk/20130401151715/https://www.education.gov.uk/publications/eorderingdownload/1471-2005pdf-en-01.pdf, © Crown Copyright 2015 Department of Education; **p.116 (Text 5): Author unknown:** from https://www.barclayslifeskills.com/downloads/organising-work-experience.pdf (2013), © Barclays bank; **p.118 (Text A): Steve Doughty:** from http://www.dailymail.co.uk/news/article-2750867/Young-people-sloppy-don-t-dress-talk-properly-Ofsted-boss-claims-teenagers-not-taught-right-skills-surviving-world-work.html (2014), © The Mail; **p.118 (Text B): Author unknown:** from http://www.myfuturesinfalkirk.co.uk/careers/main_areas_employment/top_10.aspx (2011), © 2011 My Future's in Falkirk; **p.119: Katie Roberts:** from http://www.theguardian.com/careers/careers-blog/why-i-swapped-boardroom-for-teaching (2015), Copyright Guardian News & Media Ltd 2016; **p.120: David Lodge:** from *Nice Work* (Random House, 1988), From *Nice Work* by Lodge, D., by Random House; **p.126: Lucy Kinder:** from http://www.telegraph.co.uk/news/science/10329260/The-coolest-jobs-in-the-world.html (2013), © Telegraph Media Group Limited 2013; **p.127: Benjamin Snyder:** from http://fortune.com/2015/04/15/worst-jobs/ (2015), These are the 10 worst jobs of 2015 by Benjamin Snyder; **p.129: Author unknown:** from Functional Skills English exam paper for WJEC (WJEC, 2013); **p.130: Author unknown:** from WJEC GCSE Foundation English Language paper (WJEC, 2013); **p.131: Ben Aaronovitch:** from *Broken Homes* (Gollancz, 2013), Ben Aaronovitch (2013) Broken Homes by Hachette UK; **p.132: Author unknown:** from WJEC GCSE Foundation English Language paper; **p.137: Author unknown:** from http://www.channel4.com/news/why-do-people-use-food-banks (2014), © Channel Four Television Corporation 2016; **p.138: Simon Murphy and Sanchez Manning:** from http://www.dailymail.co.uk/news/article-2608606/No-ID-no-checks-vouchers-sob-stories-The-truth-shock-food-) (2014), © Daily Mail. Used by permission; **p.141: Costas Kantouris:** from http://www.independent.ie/world-news/europe/torrential-rains-and-thick-mud-are-latest-hurdles-for-refugees-31518647.html (2015), © Independent House; **pp.142-3: Author unknown:** from http://www.savethechildren.org.uk/about-us/emergencies/child-refugee-crisis-appeal (2015), From the Save the Children Website, September 2015. Reproduced with permission of Save the Children; **p.151: Sally Williams:** from http://www.walesonline.co.uk/incoming/volunteers-who-help-make-welsh-7854731 (2014), © Trinity Mirror Publishing; **p.152 (Text B): Author unknown:** from http://www.vango.co.uk/gb/content/37-the-scout-association (2015), © Vango 2016; **p.153 (Text C): Author unknown:** from http://www.neathlittletheatre.co.uk/get-involved/4586100597 (2015), © Neath Little Theatre; **p.153: Alexander McCall Smith:** from *Love Over Scotland* (Abacus, 2006), *Love Over Scotland* by Alexander McCall Smith © **Hodder Education; p.159: Author unknown:** from WJEC Functional Skills English exam paper (WJEC, 2015); **p.160 (Text B): Author:** from WJEC Functional Skills English exam paper (WJEC, 2015); **p.160 (Text C): David Millward** (The Daily Telegraph/WJEC, Jan 2015), © Telegraph Media Group Limited 2015; **p.160 (Text D): Author unknown:** from http://www.mix96.co.uk/news/local/1693617/teens-fundraising-marathon-for-hospice-charity/ (2015), © 2016 Johnston Publishing Ltd.; **p.160 (Text E): Gregory Walton and PA:** from http://www.telegraph.co.uk/news/uknews/11098586/Courageous-Stephen-Suttons-fundraising-legacy-surpasses-5-million.html (2014), © Telegraph Media Group Limited 2014; **p.162: Author unknown:** from WJEC Functional Skills English exam paper (WJEC, 2015); **p.163 (Text B): Judith Reith (www.parentingpeople.co.uk) and Frank Furedi, Professor of Sociology:** from WJEC Functional Skills English exam paper (WJEC, 2015), Children under 15 should never drink alcohol, Government to advise parents by Daniel Martin © Daily Mail. Used by permission; **p.163 (Text C): Ellie Mae O'Hagan:** from http://www.theguardian.com/commentisfree/2012/jul/02/bangor-curfew-alienate-teenagers (2012), Copyright Guardian News & Media Ltd 2016.